S,
October 2000
a little lite read
♡ Belinda

YIN & TONIC

Yin & Tonic

Comic writing by

Renée

VINTAGE

To Bernadette, with love.

And to the Great Motivators — Harriet, Michael, Tammy, Gillian and Juliet. Also with love. First you send me a cheque which I promptly share between my overdraft and credit cards. I'll start soon, I promise myself, basking in the unaccustomed bliss of the bank manager's approving smile. Then Michael rings asking if I'd like to go to Auckland in five weeks' time to meet the reps who'll be selling the book. Very soon, I vow. Then I get a Christmas card from Harriet, Tammy, Gillian, Juliet and the aforementioned Michael saying things like, 'Can't wait to read your ms!' Shit, I thought, stomach lurching, nerves quivering, eyes staring, shit, this is serious! Better get going!

A VINTAGE BOOK
Published by
Random House New Zealand
18 Poland Road, Glenfield, Auckland, New Zealand

First published 1998

ISBN 1 86941 358 X

Cover photograph: Fleur Wickes
Printed in New Zealand by Publishing Press Limited

Contents

How's your day been? ... 7

Gnome away from gnome; or, My little green gnome in the west ... 10

Memories are made of this ... 15

Cooking with Renée I ... 18

To tell or not to tell, that is the answer ... 19

Gardening with Renée I ... 23

You too can be well developed ... 24

You say emotional, I say emotional ... 30

Cooking with Renée II ... 32

New Zealand's greatest pastime ... 33

For whom the iron steams ... 38

Real women ... 42

Eating out ... 44

Touring ... 48

Apostrophe's ... 52

That's not Portland Island Lighthouse, darling, it's moi! ... 55

Making the pizza ... 57

On hearing poems read in a pub one Thursday night ... 61

Pigeon or pear? ... 63

New Year's revolutions I ... 66

What did he mean to you? ... 67

Dear Publisher ... 71

Gardening with Renée II ... 75

The day Ernie nearly lost his wife ... 76

When I'm grown up ... 79
Talk's cheap ... 82
Gardening with Renée III ... 85
Homophobia on the range ... 86
Facts of life for lezzies ... 88
You just don't understand ... 89
Best friends? ... 91
Ladies and gentlemen ... 93
New Year's revolutions II ... 96
The sound of music ... 97
Et tu, Brute ... 101
Constance Spry and I ... 103
Camping ... 107
The good old days ... 110
An hour with... ... 111
A fairy story for baby dykes ... 113
Just popped in to cheer you up ... 120
To my two lost kilos wherever you are ... 122
Housework with Renée I ... 125
Changing the clocks ... 126
Why I like Auckland (Well hush my mouth!) ... 128
The day Mrs Ernie nearly went blind ... 133
Pet accessories ... 136
New Year's revolutions III ... 139
The night Mrs Ernie went 10 no trumps ... 140
Travelling with Renée ... 144
Is it Me? ... 146
Housework with Renée II ... 148
When I tell you I've got breast cancer ... 149
Bibliography ... 151

How's your day been?

I'll put you in the picture. I'm rushing in and out from the car which is parked in the middle of our shared driveway. I'm in a hurry because it is late afternoon and my neighbour will be home with his kids from school any minute. Quickly I unload ten bags from the supermarket. The last two clink loudly in spite of each bottle being wrapped in the three sheets of newspaper I'd insisted on. Our recycling bin is the only one in the street that ever has any empty wine bottles in it, so I am reluctant to fuel the rumours that I know are already rife: those two are lesbians, lesbians frequent bars, lesbians drink a lot, ergo ergo ergo.

As I run towards the door, pup skittering madly around my feet, I trip and crash into the table with the vase of roses and the phone on it. The water and roses splatter and spread at the speed of light all over the wooden table and the carpet, and the pup, thinking this is a new game of fetch, seizes one of the roses in her teeth and rushes out the door just as the phone rings. Concussed and in shock, I pick the damn thing up and snarl, Hello.

How's your day been? asks a strange voice. I might have known it. A Tele-Con. The voice doesn't wait for an answer, because it has really important news for me. Out of all the people in New Zealand, our household has been chosen to receive a generous gift. If they might speak to the person in the household who has just had their sixteenth birthday, is of Portuguese extraction, usually lives in the South Island, does most of the shopping and is preferably (ha ha ha) male, they'll be able to pass on the glad news. Oh, and if that person decides to accept this special offer to buy, at huge discount, a timeshare apartment in Naenae, they'll throw in a week in Waggawagga for the whole family, all expenses paid.

My neighbour has pulled up behind my car, is honking the horn and smiling patiently. His kids leap out and run down the drive. From out on the road I hear a high-pitched whine of brakes followed by some yelling in what can only be a foreign language. My pup barks joyously, another new game! The nextdoor kids screech with laughter. I see water from the tiny wee vase of roses has now covered the entire sitting-room floor.

Why is it, I ask myself, that these eager beavers always wait until I'm stressed out of my brain to give me the cheerful earful? Why don't they ring when I've parked the car neatly in the garage, put all the groceries away in the right places, given the pup a drink of water with crushed sleeping pills in it, drunk three cups of strong black coffee each with a good dollop of whipped cream and two teaspoons of white sugar, munched ten Crunchie bars one after the other, and am in the mood to be kind? Or when the moon is blue?

I have very few religious nuts knocking on the door — I have solved that problem. I pass on my never-fail tactic here for free, should you decide to use it:

1: Open the front door.

2: Give whoever's standing there a quick once over. A word of advice here. If they have kids with them, are clutching a rolled-up magazine and looking as though they've just concluded a testing session of *ex tempore* prayer — Jehovah's Witness. If they're tall, male, aged twelve, dressed in a suit and have huge tombstone teeth which they bare at you the instant you appear — Mormons. Either way they get the same treatment.

3: Say very loudly: 'You're wasting your time, I'm a lesbian feminist and it's catching, so bugger off quickly.' Then shut the door.

I like to think I inherited this skill from my mother, although I admit I've never quite reached her level of competence. A woman of few words, she only had to open the door, give one of her famous looks — a mixture of loathing, aggression, and deep contempt — and the next minute two part-time missionary positions (if you see what I mean) would be going vacant as the earnest evangelists backed off, yelling, *Not interested, not interested!*

I had won the war at the door, but I was still fighting a rearguard action over the phone. The thing is, you can't *see* who's on the other end. The phone call could be from anyone . . . Steven Spielberg . . . anyone. Well, it might.

When I moaned to my friend Titania, Tit for short, about my ineptitude, she told me about her brainwave the previous night. Do with it what you will.

Over the preceding two nights Tit had been plagued with a series of twenty-three phone calls. The next night, just as she'd settled herself on the couch, three pillows at her back, a serious gin and tonic at hand, the calls started again. She listened courteously enough as the caller promised her a holiday for six in Hokitika, first-class flights and accommodation, all expenses paid, plus one million dollars in spending money — if she could bring to the phone a short, dark, disabled heterosexual who did all the washing, who was aged thirty-seven, whose birthday was between 10 and 12 May this year and who would buy a lifetime supply of Smacko, the Game for Two with Nothing to Do, at a mere $10,000 (or three monthly instalments of $4000), freight included.

She'd hardly hung up on this offer — she hadn't even had one sip — when the phone rang again. Tit saw red. Stop being a doormat, Tit, she told herself. Remember your assertiveness training. She took a deep breath. A special prize was waiting for the tall, fair, freckled, gay male member of the household, who drove a truck and played bowls for Pukekohe. Three gold bars, a string of 100 matching pearls, tickets for two to the finals of the All Black test against South Africa in the year 2165 — all were his if he purchased the complete home gym, a snip at $50,090 with free instruction manual, delivered to the door.

Tit had remained silent all through round one, but when the Tele-Conner stopped, Tit went for it. Breathing heavily into the phone, she murmured between gasps, *Yes yes, I love it, do it again oh please do it again.* After a brief startled moment, the Tele-Conner acceded to this request and sped into round two, which was — you guessed it — a repeat of round one, with the addition of an ill-disguised tremor of anxiety. She probably thought Tit was her supervisor checking her out. Tit redoubled her efforts then switched into a series of orgasmic growls which climaxed in a high-pitched shriek, just as her caller got to the bit about the free instruction manual. Into the charged silence, Tit said huskily, *à la* Dietrich, *That was great for me — how was it for you?* There was no answer except for a slight click. Since then Tit has not heard from one single Tele-Con.

Over to you.

Gnome away from gnome; or, My little green gnome in the west

A few years ago we were out driving. It may have been a Sunday afternoon but then again it may not. Usually on Sunday afternoons we're filling the car and its boot with garden rubbish because we're going to the dump, or we're actually going to the dump, or we're gardening because next weekend we are planning to go to the dump. We make these frequent trips to the dump because we have a small section and a small garden shed which is already full to the brim with garden tools, an axe, a large spray thing you stick on your back, shelves of seeds and bulbs I'm saving for the spring, ten pairs of gardening gloves, seed boxes, bags of potting mix, seed growing mix, blood and bone, rose fertiliser, sheep manure pellets, parrot-beak pruning shears. There's even a wooden toolbox with screwdrivers (Philips and ordinary), nails, screws, hooks, a hammer and a spanner in it, but we never use these tools because we can never find the box because it's always covered over with garden rubbish. When we need a nail we look in the end compartment in the drawer above the cupboards in the kitchen, and when we find the right size, we bang it in with the handle of the axe.

Whenever we go to the dump we buy an icecream on the way back. An icecream in a cone. Whether I'm watching my diet (it may be, for instance, one of those times when I'm observing keenly all the butter, cheese and chocolate that somehow forces its way through my lips), whether we're on yet another budget, or whether it's snowing — doesn't matter. We buy an icecream. When I turn 100 and get my letter from the Queen and the silly young person from television wants to know what I'm going to do for a treat, my eyes will light up, I'll grin — perhaps vacantly, but I'll grin — and mumble, I'm going for a ride to the dump and on the way back I'll have an icecream.

So it was probably not a Sunday.

But anyway, when we were out for this ride, we saw some gnomes on a table on the grass verge. There was a large card beside them which said 'Gnomes for sale'. We stopped. Of course we stopped. Don't *you* stop when you see something for sale?

I observed, keenly again — I'm a very keen observer — that there appeared to be only male gnomes for sale. Had all the female ones been sold?

'There were no female ones.'

'What none?'

'None.'

'Why?'

The woman behind the table started to exhibit signs of irritation. She looked hopefully up the road for a car that would stop, but they all drove past.

'Because that's what the moulds were,' she said finally.

'Do you mean there are no moulds of female gnomes?'

'None.'

'None at all?'

'That's what none means.' She sounded as though she could get unpleasant very quickly, so we returned to the car and took off.

I was astounded. I had never realised till then how sexist the gnome business was. I kept my eye out after that, and sure enough, I never saw any female gnomes. This was ridiculous. I got a book from the library and there on the page was the information that only male gnomes were seen out and about, as the female gnomes were too busy staying home and looking after house and children.

'Don't take it so literally,' said my Significant Other. 'It's a joke. It's irony. Or satire.'

She's not sure of the difference and neither am I.

But I'm a humourless feminist. I take everything seriously.

Now I've never been terribly interested in garden gnomes, or garden ornaments of any kind. Maybe, if we didn't have a cat, I might be tempted by a bird bath, but that's it. But the fact that there were no female garden gnomes nagged at me. Like why the apple falls down instead of up nagged at Newton, I suppose, or the possibility of someone speaking to someone else through a piece of wire nagged at Alexander Graham Bell. I began to think, why didn't someone make some female gnomes, just to redress the balance? Then I thought, maybe *I* should. This led to a heavy political discussion.

'Why?'

'Someone should.'

'But you don't like that sort of thing.'

'I know.'

'Then why?'

'It's the principle of the thing.'

'Do me a favour!'

At the time we were living on a bigger section with two sheds, so I had the space. I got some dummies (yes, that's what the clay originals are called in the trade) made. This was a frustrating and exceedingly irritating business. This was when I confirmed something I had long suspected — that words mean different things to different people.

'I want you to make a female gnome. A short, sturdy, calm-looking gnome, in a long dress with clogs on her feet. Here is a sketch. Do you think you can do it? If so, when?'

Not so difficult to grasp, is it?

Then what's this tall, thin, worried, Barbie-like gnome in high-heeled boots doing here? And this curvaceous number with pouty lips and swirling dress?

And what about the two that exploded in the kiln?

Finally. A short, sturdy, calm-looking female gnome in one piece. Success. I asked this particular genius to make me three more. A gardener (shovel and gumboots), a healer (black bag with a red cross on it), a musician (violin in one hand). No problem.

What else did I need? Moulds. The moulds were a piece of cake because the people who made them were very skilled. The dummies got broken in the process, but hey, you can't make an omelette etc etc. Among other things I'd been told I would need was a vibrating table, so I got a friend to show me how to make one. I've heard all the witticisms, thank you.

A vibrating table is an ordinary table with a small motor attached which, when turned on, makes the table shake, which in turn makes the moulds and their innards shake and thus the concrete filling is encouraged to settle without air bubbles.

I would need a workbench, two coal shovels, a stick to poke the stuff down into the mould, paint and brushes. And I would need the makings.

So there I am with all the gears, looking nervously at four moulds, a bag of sand, a bag of cement, a vibrating table, two scrapers, a couple of buckets, and listening to my mother's voice saying, '*If you're not careful you'll end up on Queer Street.*' Fortunately the voice is drowned out by the advice given by the people who sold me the sand and cement. I can't make sense of it all, so I ring my brother-in-law who is a gun concrete-maker, and say, tell me how to make concrete. He says, what was your name again? I say, cut it out. So he tells me how to make concrete. It sounds a bit like making scones: 'Be careful when you add the liquid. You don't want the mixture too dry or too wet.'

Terrible experience, my diary records of this first pouring. *Took three hours,* I added. *Rather not go through that again.* I should tell you that these very words were written in my diary before, many many years ago — but that time they did not refer to the making of concrete. But back to the present.

The next day they came out of the moulds perfect. There was one with a largish dimple in her cheek, but to me she was perfect. The next lot fell over while they were drying, and I had an inspiration that was nothing less than brilliant. I stood the moulds in empty flower pots and this kept them secure and stable when the table vibrated. I always knew I was a genius.

I will draw a veil over the next few weeks — my sore arms, sore back, waning interest of all my friends in the riveting topic of getting the concrete mix just right. I can't understand some people's lack of interest in the world around them, can you?

The painting was fun because I got a student from Job Search to do the fine stuff like eyes and mouth. When the first four were finished and I stood them on a linen cloth on the dining table, I felt very much as Barbara Hepworth must have felt when she looked at her first finished sculpture.

And I found out a few interesting facts.

FACT 1: People with very good taste never know what to say when you invite them to look at your gnomes. This is good because they've usually got too much to say anyway.

FACT 2: People who don't care about good taste, and who sometimes put a large butterfly on the front of their house, love them.

FACT 3: People with a sense of humour want one. Immediately. They want one because they want to see their friends' faces when they show them their own personal gnome.

FACT 4: If you place two in the front of your garage they will be stolen by some marauding thieving dirty corrupt nefarious mean and nasty villain. When you ring the police to report the loss, the choked hysteria will not be just on your end of the phone.

My female gnome-making phase is over. I still have the first one with the dimple in her cheek, plus a set of four. Just to remind me. Now that there are a few in the world, I feel better. And I like to think they have made their mark. They have travelled to the far north, the deep south and middle New Zealand. Most stay where they're put, but the one in Little River keeps moving, so her owners tell me. Maybe she's a nomad, or maybe, like her maker, she gets bored easily. Or maybe she just wants someone to take her on a trip to the dump and give her an icecream on the way home.

Memories are made of this

I've just had the most wonderful experience with a repressed memory counsellor. I went to her because I hadn't slept for three years. I know, I know, Doris Lessing says writers don't sleep and yes, I've heard at least a thousand times that as I get older I need less sleep. That goes along with needing less money, less sex, less food, less pleasure of any kind from the day you turn sixty. I'm part of the generation that the guy who got free healthcare, free primary, secondary and tertiary education from our taxes, called selfish — and I suppose it is selfish to want to sleep at night, like all the real people under sixty do.

The books about insomnia all sing the same lullaby: you may *think* you didn't fall asleep until 4.30 am, but we're sure you did. (Oh yeah? And that *was* Elvis I saw walking on water at the Petone foreshore at 2.30 this morning?)

But I've tried, oh how I have tried. Let me count the ways.

Affirmations. I sleep well, I sleep well, I sleep well, I sleep well, I sleep well, dammit, whoever's listening, all you experts, I sleep well!

Meditation. I am walking down a long grey corridor stooped under the weight of a large sack I'm carrying on my shoulders. I am so tired. I stop before a closed door. I open the door and see stairs going down into a black hole. I take the heavy bag of past and present worries from my shoulder and throw it away, away, away, down the stairs, bump, bump, bump. I watch as it vanishes from sight into the black hole. Now I have no worries. I feel as light as a feather as I shut the door and walk on to another door. I open it and there is a lovely garden, flowers blooming, sun shining, birds singing. And I'm still wide awake, Buster!

The foolproof method. Even you, you sixty-year-old thicko can do this. Lights off. Lie on your back, eyes open and silently count five objects in the bedroom. Then count five sounds you can hear. Then five things you can touch. Then four, three, two, one. Just doing the countdown is fifteen objects — which is okay if you cheat and count the bed legs — but fifteen noises you can hear? Fifteen things you can touch? And then you have to start counting upwards: one, two, three, four, five. The night I tried it I was awake till six in the morning, trying to name the 33,015 things I couldn't touch, hear or see. If I ever meet the rooster who thought up this scheme, this thicko has a few words up her Minnie Dean T-shirt guaranteed to keep him awake for a few hours.

Brisk walks during the day, never at night. Okay you hordes of insomniacs who walk briskly about the streets all night, this is your leader speaking. Go home!

No rich food. I don't eat rich food. I cannot afford rich food. I am over sixty, remember?

No alcohol for an hour before you go to sleep. Are you mad?

Take a soothing bath, not hot, warm only. A warm bath? I do not find a warm bath soothing. I find a warm bath slimy, clammy, like lying in a deep well of mucus, okay?

Have a drink of warm milk last thing. Yes, you *are* mad.

Do not use your bed for anything but sleep. Oh, come on. I might be over sixty but I do not subscribe to the dictum that making love is child's play.

Calm your mind. Think only of pleasurable things. Forget the upsets of the day. Forgive anyone who has ever looked at you the wrong way. Forget that someone crashed into my car at the supermarket and didn't leave a note? Forget the cheque that didn't come? Forgive the critic who trashed a play ten years ago?

Above all, they stress, *Do not worry about not sleeping.* I don't worry about it, darlings, but I do *think* about it. Is that a crime?

Try valerian, someone advised. Valerian? The only time I tried valerian I not only stayed awake all night, eyes wide and staring, I vacuumed the house, scrubbed the shower with a toothbrush, cleaned all the windows inside and out including the upstairs ones. When the armed offenders squad arrived they were just in time to taste the wholemeal fruit bread as it came out of the oven. A few days later I read another expert who said that for some, valerian acts as a stimulant. Thank you so much.

On no account, the experts agree, *should you take sleeping pills. Your body reacts by having more sleepless nights.* So what's new? At least you get one night's deep, blissful, delightful, dreamy, rapturous, wonderful, uninterrupted sleep. Of course I know I can't go on shovelling sleeping pills down my throat; *that*'s why I went to the repressed memory counsellor, right?

But why a repressed memory counsellor, I hear you cry. Because I read about it in the advice column in a magazine I picked up at the dentist's. This woman who signed herself Darleen came out (this is how she put it, okay?) in spots every time her new boss, a veterinarian, walked into the room. Darleen was at her wit's end, hadn't slept for nights — a complete wreck. Then she read, in that very column, something about repressed memory counselling, so she thought, why not? In the first session, at $165 per hour (the scream that made the dentist's receptionist jump up and hit her knee on her keyboard was mine), she struck gold. Darleen remembered that when she was three months old she'd been frightened by a dalmatian. Problem solved. Reverse impact syndrome, the counsellor called it. Next time her boss came near, Darlene smiled, patted him on the head and said Good boy — and not a spot appeared. She just had to write and say thank you. She'd felt so good she'd gone home and slept for *twelve hours*.

Well, I thought, I've tried everything else. All right, not *quite* everything. There'd been that suggestion (I have forgiven this person) about trying triathlon training. Great for curing sleeplessness, apparently. I am sure this is true; but my fear is not that triathlon training wouldn't cure sleeplessness, but that, in my case, with my body, it would cure it forever. If you see what I mean.

So off I went to the repressed memory counsellor. I'd have to extend my mortgage and live on silverbeet and cask dregs for a fortnight, but if it worked I'd be too busy sleeping to care. And Darleen was right. It was wonderful. The curtains were drawn, the lamp lit, the chair comfort plus. I sank back into its plush velvet depths. The counsellor listened to my tale of woe. She was very concerned at my plight. She leaned towards me and I saw she had a large red suppurating pimple on the end of her nose and a cluster on each cheek. I shut my eyes.

When I woke up it was dark and I was on my own. There was a note on the desk that said, *Please leave your cheque at reception on your way out.*

COOKING WITH RENÉE 1

It's always after they have accepted your invitation to dinner that people tell you they don't eat meat, dairy, carbohydrates or white flour.

Unless you're feeling very strong and in the mood to handle disappointment, disaster and dishonour with a brilliant smile and a careless shrug of the shoulders, do not ever ever EVER choose a recipe simply because it looks so beautiful in the photograph.

Don't forget to wear your glasses when buying 300 ml cartons of cream, otherwise you can spend up to a day beating milk and it still won't thicken.

If someone asks you for the thyme, 'ten to' may not be the answer they're looking for.

If you read a recipe that includes chopped pistachio nuts among its ingredients, ignore it. There are always one or two (or twenty) pistachio nuts that will reduce your kitchen whizz to hiccuping sobs in two minutes.

If a recipe lists butter, cream, eggs, cheese (both Stilton and Cheddar) in large quantities and is combined with two cups of cooking chocolate and half a litre of white truffle oil, you can be pretty sure it won't be approved of by someone.

To tell or not to tell, that is the answer

Why is it that, for some people, just the possibility that you might be sixty or over is enough to bring on what the Victorians would call a 'spasm'? It's only six tens, after all. At a party recently, I mentioned to the woman on my left that there were several over-sixties in the stretch class that I attended, and wasn't that great? 'Ffffff!' she breathed back through clenched lips, then glared at me and hissed, 'I'm not over sixty!' 'No, but I am,' I said, giving her my best Charlie Brown sawtooth. She didn't smile back.

I knew what she was thinking: Go away. Go away. You're sixty and you're actually saying it out loud. Have you no shame? People over sixty should have a car going along in front of them with a banner that reads, not WIDE LOAD FOLLOWING, but UNCLEAN! UNCLEAN! (In my case, perhaps, we could retain the 'Wide Load' sign as well.)

Nothing about you changes the day you turn sixty. Nothing. Remember that. You don't wake up needing a hip replacement, or forgetting where you put the marbles you mislaid when your kids hit adolescence. You still get great pleasure from someone telling you they're very glad you were born. You still get stressed; you still have tantrums when life doesn't go your way. Food and cooking don't suddenly lose their charm; and when you hear old songs on the radio you still grab the cat or the dog and have a foxtrot. You still froth at the mouth when people on big wages tell other people on small wages that they're bad boys and girls for not saving. Things still matter.

What does change, though, is other people's attitudes.

One day you go into a café with your partner, and she orders a pot of Earl Grey and you order a flat white. No problem. You get served the flat white and she gets the tea. The day you turn sixty, you order a flat white and it gets offered to her. Why? Because she's not sixty, and people under sixty drink flat white and people over sixty drink tea. Got it?

When you go out to dinner at a decent restaurant, the maître d' offers his attention, information regarding specials, the wine list, the weather, who has been made prime minister, and any other choice morsels to your partner. Why? Because she's under sixty and is able to comprehend, take them all in, while you, you greedy, selfish old guzzler, are in the twilight of your life. You should just eat what's put in front of you and I don't want to hear any whinging about it, okay?

If you go to a restaurant that offers a discount for old-age pensioners, you are served what looks like yesterday's leftover roast and vegetables, and the meal's half the size even though the price is only reduced by a third.

When you're under sixty and go on a protest march, you're a caring liberal wanting to see justice done. If you're over sixty and you make a peep against the status quo, you're a grizzling geriatric.

You may laugh, all you under-sixties. Just you wait.

Take the hairdresser. Jason or Amanda asks you about your work, what you're doing for the weekend, what you think of the new prime minister, and have you thought about a change of hair colour? The day you turn sixty, the first thing Jason or Amanda says is, 'How are your grandchildren?'

When you tell them you want your hair cut fairly short because it grows so quickly they nod and smile, but as they cut your hair they leave little wisps, because wisps are feminine and, 'We don't want to get too butch, do we?' Yes, yes! I've always wanted to be really butch, but the nearest I've come is being able to change washers on taps. If I can look the part, maybe I'll be able to do a car maintenance course, ride a Harley in full leathers and Brylcreem my hair.

No wonder I seek out the salons where the hairdresser (Hi Soala! Hi Peter!) thinks I've done something more in my life than have kids who have kids. Don't get me wrong, you kids, I'm not disowning you. But I have done a few other things as well.

Unless you've been struck dumb with a severe case of tonsillitis, never NEVER go shopping with someone younger. By the time you've been into ten shops and been treated like the invisible woman, there's only one thing to do. Throw yourself against the clothes rack with a loud cry of *Germaine!* and lie there drumming your heels on the floor. Refuse all offers of help. When every assistant in the shop and those from the three shops on each side as well as over the road have finally noticed you, thresh around a bit more to cries of *Okay Gloria! Betty! Robin! This is for you!*

When you have everyone's undivided attention, rip open the plastic container in your bag and, using the underarm bowling method, toss the blue vein and fruit salad all round the shop. Making heave-ho sounds interspersed with stentorian bellows of *Kate! Marilyn! Erica!* will add to the atmosphere.

I think you'll find that next time you go into any of these shops, you will not have to complain about not being noticed.

However, like everything else, invisibility has its good side. How else could you sit at the back of the bus or in a café and hear how Zac's crop is going and when it'll be harvested, or what John did when he arrived home and discovered Betty in bed with Rob. You find out what happened to Tania and Jarrod when Tania's parents went off to a Rotary conference, and why Rosalie took to Rory's two dozen bottles of Cloudy Bay Sauvignon Blanc and his three dozen bottles of Cloudy Bay Chardonnay with a hammer. (Apparently she discovered him on the floor of the wine cellar with Pedro, the wine rep.)

You are party, from the next booth, to the discussion between two cheerful-looking men. One of them becomes aware that you could possibly overhear. You smile as though you have recently been discharged into the community. 'The old girl okay?' the friend asks. 'Can you count to 100 backwards?' asks the first one. You nod and let a dribble of flat white run down your chin. They shrug and go back to discussing whether it should be a car accident or a drive by. You wait until they've gone and then you attempt to solve the moral dilemma: should you tell someone? And if so, what will you say?

You see the scene with horrible clarity: a police interview room. You know what they're like. You've watched every episode of *The Bill* for about twenty years. There is this sixty-year-old lesbian (you have to tell them, it's probably all on the Wanganui computer anyway) telling a young, straight (presumably) cop aged twelve that she overheard two guys in a café plotting to kill someone. The cop rolls his eyes at his fellow officer (also straight, also twelve) and the interrogation begins.

'Can you describe them please, Madam?'

'Of course. One was short and fat, and the other tall and thin.'

'Age?'

(Why is he asking that? Shrug.) 'Under sixty.'

'Hair colour?'

'One was bald and one was sort of brown.'

'Clothes?'

'Jeans and grubby white T-shirts.'

‘I see. We have two men under sixty, one bald and one with sort of brown hair, both wearing grubby white T-shirt and jeans. Was there anything about them that stood out?’

‘Of course there was. They were plotting to kill someone.’

‘Thank you, Madam. Don’t call us, we’ll call you.’

GARDENING WITH RENÉE 1

A hose is always shorter than your garden.

There's never enough compost.

You *can* have too many basil seedlings.

The day you decide to dig out that lavatera which has sulked all spring, it bursts into flower.

You set out to prune a camellia so that a sparrow, should it choose to do so, can fly through the spaces between branches. While you clip away at this boring job, you plan a new rose bed full of fragrant David Austins. When you stand back you see that an adult albatross, should it venture into your garden with full wingspan extended, will experience no difficulty at all in making its way through the spaces.

A hose is always on the front path when you walk in with a case of very expensive bottles of wine.

Seeds from forget-me-nots zoom in direct flight towards any dog that happens to be passing.

Any garden looks better when it's wet. So if you have a crowd of people arriving in thirty minutes and you haven't had time to do anything to your weed-ridden, diseased, black-spotted roses, take five minutes to cut off as many deadheads as you can, then put the hoses on full bore for twenty minutes. This will probably, in the long run, add to the diseases on the leaves, but hey, in the short run, which is all you've got, your garden will look heaps better.

Never ever get all togged up in your best Ashley Fogels (because you are going to Government House for a book launch, stupid, why else?) and say, I'll just have a wander around the garden before we go.

It's all attitude, and weed is just another four-letter word. I watered and composted and talked affectionately to a clump of dear little yellow flowers for months until a passing postie told me it was oxalis.

You too can be well developed

My mother believed in self-development. She developed me all by herself. By the end of the first week into our relationship I knew when she was pleased and when she was not, and as far as she was concerned that was all I needed to know. Her influence has lasted with me to this day, and if she were alive I'd probably still be watching her to work out my moves. *Is she in a good mood? She is. Good. I'll ask if I can go to the pictures.*

A good mood? Are you mad? Forget the pictures.

My mother was the first in a long queue of people who have wanted to develop me. They are dying to help me reach my full potential, foster my creativity, become my own person, discover what colours my aura might be, rid myself of all nasty thoughts, improve my mental and emotional health, save my soul. All I have to do is place myself, plus a few hundred dollars, into their hands. The save-my-soulers like it in small amounts each week — sort of your ten per cent hire-purchase salvation, it's not yours until you've made the last payment, and if you do the flowers each week you'll get an extra star in your crown — but the others prefer the lump sum right at the beginning. So handy — they're not the ones who are out of pocket when it doesn't work.

Forgiving people will make you feel better, swears one of these gurus jostling for my attention. Fred Forget-Me-Not looks at me seriously from the front of the brochure which shows him full-face as well as in profile. Flowers of Forgiveness is one of the cheaper workshops. In two hours, Fred promises, I'll be a new person: all the horrible hurts, ugly upsets, psychic bruises that I carry with me into each day will be gone. All for a small fee plus two hours of my time. Why not, I think. Fred looks a trustworthy chap. And it'll help pass the time while I wait for the postie to bring a cheque.

While Fred looks on, I make my first call.

'Hello, is that Dymeter?'

'Who wants to know?'

'It's Renée.'

'Renée who?'

'I'm just ringing to say I forgive you.'

'If you're trying to sell me something, forget it.'

Or I can ring people and ask them to forgive me.

'Hello?'

'Hi Jacaranda, it's Renée. I'm just ringing to ask your forgiveness. I'm sorry I lost my temper at your twenty-first birthday party thirty years ago and threw your cake out the window which happened to be closed at the time. But you shouldn't have chucked your blackberry nip down my new white top that took me three days to pintuck and a week to make. That was why I jumped up and down and tore the top off. I wasn't trying to draw attention to myself and spoil your party. How could you think I was that sort of person? I was hurt, Jacaranda, and hurt people do strange things.'

'Are you going to pay for the window?'

I give a gay (I know, I know!) laugh.

'Piss off, then.'

'Thank you Jacaranda, I feel better now.'

I pay Fred and walk out into the bright day, a sadder and wiser woman. Also poorer. Long-distance calls are not included in the fee and, like some motel owners, Fred works on a system I'm sure Telecom would like to hear about. He charges double for long-distance calls made on holidays. Well, it's not for the call, he explains, it's the administration system he shares with his neighbour, who owns a motel. Told you.

I like the idea of the primal scream workshop, which is called, unsurprisingly, Twist and Shout. For a small fee I can shout and rant and jump up and down and beat hell out of a cushion which is standing in for someone who should be there. I can scream at the government, curse the Pope, swear at my mother (like hell, I'm not prepared to risk that, she's only been dead fifty years), all in complete security and safety, while my tutor, one Mary Smith, looks on benignly, urging me on when I falter or drop with exhaustion. But I decide to say no. After all, I can do this for a nominal door charge on Friday nights at any club or party.

I can relive the moment of my birth: *Aah! Aaah! Christ why did I do it? I'll kill the bugger! Never again! Aaah!* I think not.

I can indulge in a weekend of co-counselling, which is where I and another equally wounded person tell each other our troubles, the principle being that both of us will feel better knowing we are not the only ones in the world who suffer in this way. We will be able to support each other because we will both understand the agony the other is going through.

I'm not too impressed by this rationale. It seems to me that by the time a distraught person has spilled out their rage, bitterness, and desire for revenge on someone who used to be their nearest and dearest, and who, on the eve of their trysting ritual had run off with the milkwoman, they don't actually want to hear about someone else's bitterness, resentment and desire for revenge, ditto. If I'm going through a hard time I couldn't care less about yours. It's all me me me. I'm sorry, but there it is.

A course called Fostering Your Creativity appealed to my friend Tit. She liked the idea put forward in the brochures that all human beings are born with creative talent, but somehow or other it gets repressed, constrained, confined, as we battle for our daily bread (yes, all right, said Tit, catching my eye). Creativity is all around us, just waiting to be seized. We should fill our (metaphorical) goblets to the brim and drink. In a few weeks we could be up there with the greats.

All Tit had to do was cough up $1200 and spend three hours a week for six weeks with Frank McGluskey and Ernestine Dooley, tutors and originators of Fostering Your Creativity, at their Herb Farm retreat, and she too would join the ranks of the successful writers, painters and craftspeople who have become household names. What was $1200, compared to the fortunes she would be making in six months' time when, her creativity well and truly fostered, she too stepped into the limelight?

Tit said she should have listened to the notes of caution coming thick and fast through the ether in her mother's voice. Her mother was in Hawaii having a holiday with her man of the moment, Chunky Dogg. *The verb*, her Mum's voice screeched operatically around her neurons, *The verb!* The verb? The doing word? What on earth can it mean? thought Tit. You're imagining things, she told herself, and felt a wash of pleasure. It's starting to work already, she thought, and I've only just read the brochure.

She had two questions for Frank and Ernestine. One, could she pay off the $1200 in weekly instalments? And two, if their course was so good, why hadn't she heard the names Frank McGluskey and Ernestine Dooley in connection with the arts?

Tit thought they must have been asked these two questions before, because their answers came very fast. Yes, she could pay in weekly instalments, but there would be an administrative fee of $500. As for the second question, Frank and Ernest (as she liked to be called, apparently) regarded themselves as channels via whom creativity rolled, like a volcanic lahar in a starry sparkling stream, to their students. Creativity on their part would not only subvert the higher calling they were here in this poor old world to follow ('Yes, all right!' said Tit, 'this is how they talked, okay?') but would also result in dismal failure. Those who can, teach, and those who can't, do, they said profoundly.

So she signed up. Six weeks later she realised what her mother had been screeching about. Fostering her creativity had more to do with assisting Frank and Ernest in slugging back a daily liquid lahar of a certain beverage than with nurturing Tit in her struggle to release the Frances Hodgkins in herself. However, all was not lost. When faced for the sixth time with a couple of merry, red-faced tutors who told her that, if she signed up for just one more course, one day she would see her paintings hung in exhibitions just like her idol FH, Tit became very creative — not with paints, but with words. I can't repeat them, however, although I can say that a few of them started with F followed by another starting with H (and they didn't sound like Frances Hodgkins).

My last go at developing myself was little better than Tit's experience. I've always been very possessive about books. Let's rephrase that: I'm a real greedy-guts where books are concerned. I read all the reviews and want every one — even the ones that get bad reviews. Especially the ones that get bad reviews. Why is that, I wonder? I also admit, between you and me, that courses that promise to take in the tired, repressed, depressed, guilt-ridden, anti-social, aggressive old me and, after a weekend, a month, six weeks, turn out a lively, exuberant, happy, guiltless, party-person, peace-loving new me have a certain attraction, however much I may scoff.

So when I get a chance to kill two birds with one stone — that is, buy a book which promises all the things a self-development course offers, but which can be read in private for the price of just the book — I'm there.

'SOB Your Way to a Better You', said the ad. A revolutionary new system invented by Silver Dawn Morning, Counsellor, Carer, Mother of Ten and now Author of a Bestseller. Apparently Silver Dawn Morning had been treating friends, family and assorted forlorn folk for some years before being persuaded to put pen to paper, tactile member on typewriter, claws on keyboard, as the case may be.

The result is her book, entitled *SOB You!* Based on the collected wisdom of ancient lore and myth mixed with all the best of the World's Great Religions and Philosophies as studied by Silver Dawn Morning in the reaches of the night when she was tending to her Little Ones and sifted through Silver Dawn's own natural intelligence and fount of human kindness, this book will Change Your Life! Only $250 at all good bookstores.

I looked in the morning paper. Sure enough Silver Dawn's opus had achieved a bad review. That did it. I was down to the bookstore before you could say tacky, jumping-on-the-bandwagon, new age trash. Thank God I'd refused that dinner invitation. Now I could settle in with *SOB You!* and come Monday, I'd be a new person.

I could hardly wait to get home with my book. Luckily I'd managed to get to the shop in time to yank the last copy from the hands of the little old man who'd been waiting since early morning for the shop to open. Now it was between me and Silver Dawn Morning.

The *SOB You!* Way of Life, said Silver Dawn Morning in her first sentence, means that from this moment on, Inner Tensions will no longer wear and tear at your Outer Self creating Disharmony which inevitably leads to mental, physical and emotional disarray. No, from this day on your inner and outer selves will merge and be as one in a Harmonious Whole because you will be committed to Silver Dawn's Six-Star Strategy, based on the principles of SOB.

SOB stands for the Six Stars of Your Very Own Solar System. The names of these stars are Share, Shake, Order, Open, Beautify and Bond.

Here is the Renée's Digest condensed version of Silver Dawn Morning's Six-Star Strategy for Self-Development, or *SOB You!*

First Star — Share. Share your worry, your fear, your happiness, your success. Share them with neighbours, friends, strangers, the trees, the birds and the flowers by saying out loud the three things you hate most and the three things you love most. Encourage others to join in. They may be surprised at first, but persist. Rome was not built in a day.

Second Star — Shake. Shake all your old worries and anxieties away. Shake from side to side then from top to toe. Every hour on the hour. Not only will you rid your inner nerve centre of all the accumulated tensions built up over the years, you will bring a smile to the kind faces of strangers.

Third Star — Order. Every morning on waking, order your day. You want a calm happy cheerful day. Just order it! Say in loud confident tones, *Give me a happy cheerful day!* Repeat this for the time it takes you to shower and dress. Say it to your partner, your flatmates, your parents. If you have time, ring up your relatives and friends. You will be astounded at the reaction of those around you and thrilled at their efforts to make your order come true.

Fourth Star — Open. Open others to the New You. Show them how your happiness is increasing. Introduce them to the Six-Star Strategy.

Show by your openness how the distance between your inner and outer selves is being decreased by your daily practice of SOB You!

Fifth Star — Beautify. This is perhaps the simplest of the Star-based strategies but its influence is universal. Remember — Stars don't change with every new whim, Stars just Are! You can make the world and yourself more beautiful just by repeating *Stars Are!* at intervals. You will be touched and moved by the response of those around you as their starved souls accept this simple but profound message.

Sixth Star — Bond. Bond with the universe. Take every opportunity to become one with the natural world. It is not enough to feel the grass between your feet, to clasp the trees to your breast, to greet the weather, be it rain or shine, with equanimity, grace, and of course, pleasure. These things are important BUT what about the agony of nails through wood that was once a tree? What about the anguish of the grass as it is cut off in its prime? How can we measure the pain of the earth as it is cut off from the sun by a brick path? To Bond with the universe you must allow the pain as well as the pleasure to enter your Self. Accept that Bonding does not come for free. There are responsibilities. Let the tears of the earth, the tortured scream of the pierced trees, the mournful wail of the grasses be heard through you.

Well I gave it a go. By the time I'd shared my worries and fear, shaken every hour, ordered my day in a very open way, repeated *Stars Are!* while giving utterance to the pain of the path and the fear of the fence, I was exhausted. I can't say I noticed that my Inner Tension had come to terms with my Outer Self, or that I felt a new me developing from the old. What I did notice, though, was that everyone was giving me funny looks. Call me old-fashioned, but the funny looks made me feel funny. I could feel enormous amounts of Inner Tension building inside me.

Enough, I said. *SOB You!* I said to Silver Dawn Morning and snuggled thankfully into the familiar maelstrom of my Inner Tensions fighting and struggling with my Outer Self. It's my party and I'll sigh if I want to.

You say emotional, I say emotional

'And now we're going to hear from Francine Sparrows-Hoop Brown, our Court Affairs reporter, who will speak to us from outside the High Court in Wellington, where inside, today, there were emotional scenes. Good morning Francine.'

'Hello Aubrey, this is Francine Sparrows-Hoop Brown reporting from outside the High Court in Wellington where inside, today, there were emotional scenes. We're into the third day of the trial of a man charged with murdering ten people at the Chardonnay Creek Holiday Camp on Christmas Day in 1996.'

'What happened today, Francine?'

'Well Aubrey, as I said there were emotional scenes.'

'Would you like to fill the listeners in, Francine?'

'Thank you Aubrey. Well, today the mother of the accused took the stand.'

'How did she look, Francine?'

'She looked pale and emotional, Aubrey.'

'How was the accused, Francine? Did he look pale and emotional too, Francine?'

'No, as a matter of fact, Aubrey, the accused looked at his mother then looked at the ceiling then burst into song.'

'Burst into song, Francine?'

'Yes, Aubrey, song. "Hi Ho, Hi Ho, It's off to clink we go," actually.'

'So, Francine, you would say the accused was not particularly downcast.'

'No, not particularly, Aubrey.'

'Now Francine, tell the listeners about the emotional scenes.'

'Well, Aubrey, the accused's mother, who has owned and run the Chardonnay Creek Holiday Camp for ten years, said that she'd tried to get her son committed because he was showing signs that he'd taken himself off his medication. At the Chardonnay Creek Hospital she was told she must stop being overprotective. She agreed, under questioning from defence counsel, that she was anxious about her son but did not agree that she was overly anxious.'

'I'll just interrupt the flow for a brief moment here Francine. I'm sure the listeners are aware, but just in case, could you refresh our memories? This family had suffered a terrible tragedy three days prior to the shootings, I believe.'

'Yes Aubrey. They had suffered a terrible tragedy when, three days before Christmas 1996, on the 22nd of December to be exact, the accused's father had been killed in a car accident.'

'That must have been a difficult time for them. Emotionally I mean.'

'Emotionally, yes, Aubrey.'

'Now you were saying, Francine?'

'As I was saying Aubrey, the accused's mother was turned away from the hospital. When they got back to their home situated at the hilly end of Chardonnay Creek Holiday Camp, the son went to his room and didn't appear until Christmas morning when he rushed into his mother's bedroom waving a .22 rifle. He told her that all the people at the camp were devils who had gathered at Chardonnay Creek to have a conference before they took over the world. He had been given a mission from God to rid the planet of these evildoers. The mother struggled with the son for possession of the gun, but the son ran off and shot ten people before being (as the police witness said earlier) apprehended. At this point, Aubrey, the witness became very emotional.'

'Very emotional, Francine?'

'Yes Aubrey, very emotional. In fact, she broke down.'

'She broke down, Francine?'

'Yes Aubrey. The judge and counsel were shocked, and I noticed one or two of the jurors looked surprised.'

'The jury looked surprised, Francine?'

'Yes, Aubrey, and the accused's mother had to be helped from the box.'

'And Francine, tell me, what was the demeanour of the accused during this time?'

'Well, it was rather strange, Aubrey — he appeared totally impassive.'

'Totally impassive, Francine?'

'Totally, Aubrey.'

'Oh. Well. Thank you Francine. That was our court reporter Francine Sparrows-Hoop Brown reporting on the emotional scenes from the High Court in Wellington.'

COOKING WITH RENÉE II

Butter is wrapped in stuff that looks like the paper we used to save to line baking tins but isn't, so it's no use trying to line baking tins with it because it crackles and rips into small pieces which stick to the tin, the bench, the taps, your hands and the cake.

Recipes from famous cooks always leave something out. I'm not for one minute saying that this is on purpose, only that something happens between the recipe's run from table-top to typesetter. Take the recipe for grilled vegetables with a lemon juice and oil sauce I've just read. Nowhere did it list onions (red, spring or even untrendy old white) even though there were large slices of both green and white onions in full view in the photograph. What does this mean?

Is an egg really a hen's period?

Cookery books are on a par with gardening books: the greatest light romantic read you're ever going to experience.

New Zealand's greatest pastime

No, it's not rugby, racing or beer. It's not sex, going out to restaurants, or reading books. It's not going to the theatre, opera or ballet. It's not even bowls.

This pastime is indulged in by people of either sex, with people of their own or the other sex, and takes place both in the privacy of their own home and/or on the streets. It is enjoyed by people of any age. It is not a special feature of any culture, a plank of any particular political party or religious group. It is not confined to a certain class or income bracket, or whether you have or have not had children, a mammogram or cervical smear, or been tested for AIDS. It doesn't matter whether you do it in the latest Porsche or in a rusty old Ford Falcon stationwagon. Policemen do it, drug dealers do it. Politicians do it, so do poets. Women do it, men do it, kids do it. Even animals have been known to do it.

Hands up anyone who has moved house in the last five years.

There are two ways to look at this phenomenon. You can say we're a nation of nomads and wanderers who like challenges; or you can say we're a nation of masochistic idiots.

Who but a bunch of masochists would happily shove all their worldly goods into cardboard cartons, without putting labels on them, and trundle them onto a trailer hired from the local garage for ten dollars a half day, knowing they have to have it back on time because it's needed for some other fools who are moving on the same day, and there's not a hope in hell they'll be finished by midday?

And why? Because you want a bigger house, a better location, to be near your parents (oh yeah?). Because you want to get away from your parents (that's more like it), or you feel like a change (oh really?). The fact is, you would never ever think of moving, it would never enter your head, not even for one minute, unless someone close to you set the ball rolling. I refer here to your neighbour.

Have you ever walked or driven down a street and noticed that, hello, someone's selling their house? The next day you see three people are selling. By the week's end the whole street has got For Sale notices on the front fence and they're advertising bus tours to the open homes.

This is the lemming principle. Just as the small arctic rodents of that name launch themselves off a high cliff simply because the one in front has done the same, so we move house following the same deep imprinted instinct. It always surprises me that real estate agents haven't caught on to this and adopted the name: 'Lemmings Real Estate – We Leap with You!'

'Edwin, I see the Joneses are moving.'

'You'd better get over to the dairy and see if they've got any spare cartons then, Elsie.'

What else but a profound primeval urge would make people get into a car that's smaller than its towbar, towing a trailer that has not only the aforementioned cardboard cartons, dotted about in uneven heaps on top of a queen-sized bed, but also a dresser with six drawers, a fridge, and a washing machine, all tied on with a piece of garden twine wrenched off the nearest tomato stake? These people then drive like lunatics towards a house that's practically a duplicate of the one they've left. On the way they pass the previous owners of said house, trailer lurching behind them, on their way to the house just vacated by the first lot. I know, I know, there are removal firms who will allegedly take all these worries off our shoulders, but then you're faced with unpacking the bowl of cherry pips and the half-eaten pizza.

As well as those of us who engage in this activity, there is an outer ripple of people who depend on us doing it. Real estate agents, lawyers, valuers, tenancy managers, moving firms, catteries, kennels — you name it, there's hardly a profession or trade which doesn't rely heavily on the fact that we are a nation of people addicted to moving house. Think of the electricians, washing-machine people, computer salespeople, curtainmakers, those who rip up carpet that doesn't go with the new owner's furniture and replace it with carpet that won't match the next owner's furniture. How many columns of newspapers would be left bare, were it not for the houses for sale or rent advertisements? What about the doctors and nurses who tend the cuts and bruises, the broken arms and ankles; the osteopaths and chiropractors who pat and pummel and manipulate the bad backs, the dislocated shoulders, the strained muscles? Not to mention the police officers who patrol the roads, looking for the absent-minded ones who have not renewed their trailer registrations.

Forget about systems, capitalist, communist or socialist. Forget about

MMP, party politics, art and religion: it's moving house that keeps this country in business.

I for one have played my part in keeping New Zealand afloat. Many times. While all the occasions have been traumatic, one in particular stands out. This time we were moving from a rented house to one which the bank was kindly allowing us to live in, in exchange for which we were to hand over enormous sums of money on a regular basis. They, with a touch of their very own alchemy, change the cash into something called interest. This means it takes twenty years longer to pay off the house than it would if they called it money. These magicians are another group of people who couldn't remain solvent without us.

This time I was determined everything would go smoothly, so I labelled every carton, numbered them, and wrote the number and contents on a piece of paper. I haunted the lawyer's office, determined the settlements — there were three involved — should go through as in the domino theory. I arranged with Flash Gordon, the owner of the house we were buying (don't blame me, blame his father — I've met his mother and she's very protective of her son so the name couldn't have been her doing) to move out on settlement day, leaving the house clear and clean for us to move in the next day.

Flash asked if he could leave the keys in the letterbox. He had only one set and it seemed like a waste of money to get a new lot when he wouldn't need them again after that day. We agreed. Silly old us.

The settlements were paid over as planned. That day was brilliantly fine, still and calm, not a cloud in the sky. Next day, our moving day, we woke at 4.30 to the sounds of a southwesterly driving torrential rain against the windows. When my Significant Other and I looked out the window, fog obscured everything. We promised each other we would not allow these extraneous matters to mar the move to our dream house. We swore to remember that it is not what happens to us that counts, it's our attitude towards these things. We made a cup of tea and got cracking.

We arrived at the new house to find no keys in the letterbox; and yes, all the doors were locked. I looked upstairs through the gloom. Surely that was an open window? Fired by the fervour that only people engaged in this particular pursuit — or being chased by an avalanche — can know, I climbed up on the highest part of the trailer, then onto the roof overhanging the front porch, and slithered along to the windowledge, through the window and into the house.

All Flash's furniture appeared to be *in situ*. It had been shoved to one side of each room, but it was still there. I opened the ranchsliders downstairs and, in silence, thinking about attitudes, no doubt, we stacked the first trailer load of our stuff on the opposite side of the sitting room from Flash's lot. Luckily I'd packed the teapot, tray, cups, and makings in a separate carton, so we decided to have a cup while we were waiting for Flash to turn up. We both smiled cheerfully. At every opportunity.

We'd had one cup and were just starting on the refill when Flash arrived in his rusty old car which was belching black smoke that didn't quite obscure the Greenpeace sticker on the back.

'Problems,' Flash said. 'Couldn't get into the new house. Had to leave the washing machine and fridge standing in the pouring rain. Some people,' he said, shaking his head.

'Thought you were moving yesterday,' I said, forgetting to smile cheerfully.

'I had a few problems,' said Flash.

I took a deep breath. I would not, repeat not, I told myself, point out to Flash that the biggest problem he had could be seen in the mirror any time he cared to look.

Flash's mother was with him. A frail, grey-haired woman in a floral dress, a black and white spotted pinny and lambswool slippers, she looked vaguely in our direction, then marched over, grabbed two of our cartons and made for Flash's trailer.

'Hey,' I said, but caringly — she was older than me, after all — 'that's ours.'

'Oh, right,' she said, putting them back and grabbing another two from our pile plus the tray with the teapot and cups.

'So are those.'

'Oh, right.' She grabbed a box of pillows.

My partner shook her head at me. 'Let her have them,' she mouthed.

The day went from worse to worse. By nightfall, Flash's Mum had shifted most of his stuff as well as, we discovered later, a third of ours. Flash could only manage lighter articles because he had a bad back. He asked would we mind if he left the Rhode Island Reds until tomorrow because Mum would find it a bit difficult catching them in the dark. At that stage I would have agreed to look after a lioness and her newborn cubs in our bed, if it meant we would not see Flash or indeed his mother again that day. So off they went, leaving us frustrated, irritable, with the beds to put up, blankets and duvets to find, plus responsibility for half a dozen red chooks. I shone the torch into the fowlhouse and counted five sitting on a rail. 'Okay,' I snarled. 'Listen to me. We have you surrounded. Come out now, or one of your mates takes a quick trip to the oven.' There was a rustle and something that sounded like my ex-drama teacher being sick, then the missing one edged its way out of the darkness and fluttered up onto the rail. 'That's better,' I said, and clicked off the torch.

Back in the house attitude was giving way to the age-old questions asked at these times: *What am I doing? Why am I here? Who am I?*

'Thought you numbered and labelled everything and then wrote it all down on a bit of paper?'

'Flash's Mum took that too.'

Time for something stronger than tea. After some more aggressive opening of cartons with a nail I found on the drive, the Stanley knife having disappeared (yes, yes, either Flash's Mum or a passing magpie, you choose), I located some bottles of wine. I looked and looked for the carton which held the bottles of cheap plonk we'd bought on special at the local supermarket, but all I could find were the three bottles of Cloudy Bay Sauvignon Blanc, which were the basis of our superannuation investments. Bugger that, I thought. At this rate I won't be worrying about super anyway. I'll swing for Flash's murder long before then.

Fortunately the opener was in my pocket. Some things you don't leave to chance.

After an hour or two our moving day finished off much as it began. In the distance I heard the southwesterly driving torrential rain against the windows . . . but this time, happily, the fog which obscured the unpacked cartons, the duvets and the blankets, was inside and we were doing okay thank you very much, secure in the knowledge that, yet again, we had kept this country afloat for one more day.

For whom the iron steams

Welcome to the Bonding With Your Iron seminar. I think I can promise you a time of insight, inspiration and illumination.

I have been told that I'm ahead of my time. Be that as it may — there always has to be one, doesn't there? — let me share my thoughts with you. I know, yes I say this firmly, I know what the next revolution is going to be. I'm letting you in on the act because, well, I'm like that. It's my nature. I try to help people. Whether they want help or not doesn't come into it because I have found that most people do not know when they need help. So this is where I step in.

Now I'm aware that one of your longstanding repressed griefs is that you've never quite managed to get ahead of the game. You're always a follower, never a leader. You hide this deep psychological bruise with a gay smile (well maybe not exactly gay, merry perhaps) and you think no one knows your secret. Alternatively, perhaps you've repressed these feelings so successfully that you don't even know you've got them.

Never fear. Help is at hand. I will be with you all the way. I am here to say that you too can have your hour in the sun. You too can lead the way. Now I want you to close your eyes and breathe slowly and deeply, in, out, in, out, while you reflect on my next statement. Are you ready? All eyes shut? Here we go.

Ironing is the next In thing.

I'll repeat that.

Ironing is the next In thing.

You may scoff. No doubt there were scoffers when Coco Chanel launched her first long cardie. They didn't mock for long. There were, no doubt, sniggerers at the launches of Buzzy Bee, Marmite and Swanndri, but look what happened to them. Icons, my dears, icons.

Yes, you may jeer, you may quibble, but there's one thing of which you can be absolutely certain. The very last thing you would expect to become the latest fashion or fad, suddenly does. How else do you explain bouffant hairdos? Communes? Expense accounts? Credit cards? Grunge? If I'd told you five, three, even one year previously that any of these crazes would sweep the nation, you wouldn't have believed me.

Still reluctant? I know, I know, ironing has had a bad press.

Sorree!

Let's look at what the critics say then.

Irons were invented by men who wanted to give women something to do on Tuesdays. So irons are out. Wrinkles rule, okay?

Think again Buster. As far as I'm concerned, wrinkles come soon enough, without inviting them in unnecessarily. And we don't frown on electricity just because a guy called Ben invented it, do we?

Ironing is old-fashioned, you say. So, my friends, is snogging, bonking and drinking wine. If we're using old-fashioned as an excuse, let's get rid of them too.

Yes, I thought that might get your attention.

Ironing is a waste of time. This is the most serious misrepresentation of all. Think of all the essential things you can do while you're ironing. You can plan what you'll say to the boss next time she's late for your performance review. You can think up some pithy answers for the next time your cousin and her family of ten arrive just on lunchtime and you have only two slices of bread in the house:

'Have you eaten? We have.'

'Sorry, can't stop, just leaving for Botswana.'

Or you can meditate. Just choose your mantra. *Iron* is one that springs to mind. *Iiiiron yeah, iiiiron yeah*. Keep it going. *Iiiiron yeah, iiiiron yeah*. Before you know it you'll have done a full-blown, three-hour, out-of-body meditation. And you'll be right down to the bottom of the ironing basket. Yes, even that awful black satin shirt with the frills all down the front and round the collar. And you, you will feel great! What if the kids have wrecked the house? The dog's eaten your new shoes? Your partner arrived home with six colleagues who all want to party? You will greet them with a big happy smile and a look in your eyes that tells them you've been far far away in another world. Believe me, one look at you and all desire to party will disappear instantly, the kids will immediately begin picking up the chairs and duvet tunnels and the dog will take herself to her kennel where she will lie and have a really good think about life.

Think of the perfect excuse you've got when someone rings up and asks you to go to the Change Your Aura at Home workshop, the Aerobics Above the Clouds, Sixty is Just the Start session, the Rage can be Righteous rendezvous or the Standup Comedy for Those Who Like to Sit Down seminar. Just smile and say thanks for your wonderful/exciting/stimulating invitation, but you'd like to share with them your commitment to ironing. You're sure they'll understand. And they will.

Ironing is hard, you mumble? *Living* is hard, for God's sake — why blame it all on ironing?

Still not convinced? Let me tell you how good ironing is for my creative juices. It's amazing how my mind immediately whizzes into high gear the minute I start. My brain can scarcely contain the ideas that tumble and froth about in it. You're worried about how you can go out to dinner and still stick to your budget? In two seconds your problem is solved. Go out tonight and fast for the rest of the week. Simple.

I bet the reason Beethoven wrote *Fidelio*, which happens to be his only opera (I know this because I heard someone on National Radio say so) was because when he was zooming away ironing his frilly shirts (very tricky), his fingers kept getting in the way of the iron. *Zoom zoom ouch! Zoom zoom aah!* Very operatic, I'm sure you'll agree.

Katherine Mansfield, being a true New Zealand Woman, was probably ironing her best jacket when the idea for *The Doll's House* leapt into her mind. Remember the closing line? 'I seen the little light'? I rest my case.

The choreography for *Swan Lake*, I have no doubt, was inspired by fluffy heaps of white sheets; and as for Rubens, well, it's obvious he got his models to whip their clothes off so he could have a quiet iron, rather than the commonly held belief that he wanted to consider their lush curves. You may be right. It seems kinky to me too. But even artists kink occasionally. So I am told.

You don't need to pay a fortune for some young twitchy number in blue and gold lycra to leap around in front of you yelling insults when you don't jump high enough to touch the ceiling. You don't need a personal trainer for your weightlifting experience. You don't need to ring an 0800 number and add to an already overloaded credit card. You have the means to exercise right in your very own home. Your iron.

Ironing doesn't have to be austere. Forget the old tracksuit. Make it an event. Indulge yourself. Slide into something soft and flowing; or if it's very hot, maybe liberate yourself from clothes entirely, pop your favourite CD on, set up the ironing board, fill the iron with water and go for it! I guarantee ironing will never be the same again.

Word will spread. I can see it now. You'll be asked to give demos in supermarkets; editors of women's magazines will sit on your doorstep until you promise to give them an exclusive; and there'll be a ring from Oprah. Photographs of you with your trusty iron will appear on every cover. And the headlines! *Ironer Steams Ahead! Presses Her Own Suit!* And you'll have the glowing consciousness that comes with the knowledge that, at last, you are the one leading the charge in this social revolution.

And all because you discovered what it means to Bond with your Iron.

And just think, you'll never have to wear Crimplene again.

Real women

Real women shave their legs and under their arms, pluck the hair off their faces and wax away their pubic hair because they want everyone to know they're real women.

Real women believe the articles in women's magazines because they wouldn't print them if they weren't true, would they?

Real women love their periods because once they start menstruating it means they can now be a mother. Yippee!

Real women never raise their voices because someone might think they're a radical feminist.

Real women love their children even when they're shitting their pants, spewing in their bed, or screaming drunk after a School-C-exams-are-over party.

Real women can't function properly without a man to tell them they look wonderful.

Real women don't mind when their husband bonks other women because that's what men do.

Real women think it's funny when their husband wants to take a turn with the kids or hang the washing out, because that's women's work.

Real women don't find it strange that their husband comes home late three nights out of four and says he's been (a) working, (b) playing Monopoly with some friends, or (c) visiting his mother, because they trust him implicitly.

Real women prefix each sentence with *My husband. My husband says that people on the dole are just bludgers. My husband says that we should rip up the Treaty and start again.* (You mean everyone go back where they came from and start negotiations from scratch? Oh goody!)

Real women don't have deep voices because only men and lesbians have deep voices.

Real women never have morning sickness because morning sickness is all in the mind.

Real women don't care about orgasms because as long as their man is pleased they're happy.

Real women don't make a fuss when their husband gives them a black eye because he says he loves them, really.

Real women think 'masturbate' is what you have to do when the butcher gives you tough steak.

Real women wouldn't dream of missing *Coronation Street* because it gives them something to talk about when their husband comes home late.

Real women have long hair. It might be lank as hell, but it's long.

Real women think Mills & Boon novels are how life is meant to be and if they'd only been called Dorinda they'd have met someone called Blake and lived happily ever after.

Real women always laugh at jokes about women's bodies and about mothers-in-law because if they don't, everyone will think they're politically correct feminists or even (*quelle horreur!*) politically correct lesbian feminists.

Real women think you should grow old gracefully because otherwise your family will be embarrassed.

Real women die real quietly and hardly anyone notices.

Eating out

It is a truth universally acknowledged that the fewer the patrons, the poorer the service.

I wish I'd remembered this when I walked past the latest hot restaurant and saw that it was packed to the doors: patrons were trailing out onto the footpath, and a fight had broken out between two of them because one had attempted to jump the queue. Inside, all was action. Such quick service, such courtesy, such smiles. Under such stress and strain. I was so impressed, I forgot the golden rule and invited my someone special to share our anniversary meal there with me.

When we arrive, the restaurant is empty except for the staff and a group of four tourists from Monterey. We know they're from Monterey because while we're waiting to be seated in this empty restaurant, they have the time to tell us their names, where they're from, how long they've been in New Zealand and how long they'll be staying.

We are seated, and the six of us continue our wait. We listen while one member of the serving staff tells her colleagues about how, last night, her flatmates arrived home at three with two gang members, how they sang 'Ten Guitars' ('My Gard,' says someone from Monterey) until six, whereupon they all had breakfast and ate all the eggs, yes of course they were free-range, what do you think I am? How her mother called in at seven with her ironing and one of the gang members recognised her as his teacher in the fourth form and reminded her that on the questionnaire she asked them to fill in, next to ambitions he'd put Mongrel Mob member and he was here to say his ambitions had been achieved, all because of her advice all those years ago.

Then, because it's only fair and if you tell me I tell you, that's how the game is played, her workmates describe what happened after she left work last night, how the chef threw a wobbly, along with some plates and a pizza, and chased the bar manager into the storeroom brandishing a bunch of mizuna in a very threatening fashion. It all ended up happily, though, over a couple of bottles of rough red from Gisborne, and now the chef and the manager have decided to go steady.

Around now the wine waiter becomes conscious of our presence. Perhaps it's my vitriolic glares piercing her shoulder blades? Perhaps it's because someone from Monterey starts a slow clap? She smiles wearily at the others: God, people are such a drag. As she ambles slowly over to our table someone presses the play button and the restaurant is filled with the sound of people smashing a car to pieces with their bare hands and screeching about it from time to time.

'Be with you in a minute,' she tells the tourists from Monterey, while the ten workmates she's left continue their consciousness-raising session.

'Sorry, we're out of that one,' she mouths. 'Very popular one, that one.'

'Then why don't you order more?'

She smiles uncomprehendingly.

'Could you turn it down?'

'Pardon?'

I try sign language and, sighing heavily, she signals to someone. The sound relief is marginal.

We finally choose a Chardonnay which no one in their right mind would ever order, but there's a good supply and I think we might need it.

'Maybe we should go.'

'It has to get better. And the food's supposed to be really good.'

We settle in to study the menu while the tourists from Monterey fail to order the wine of their first choice and settle for the same as us.

The wine arrives. She pours a little into a glass. It's fairly dire but I indicate she should go ahead and fill the glasses. She gestures with her head at one of her colleagues who trots over to the tourists from Monterey, while another one heads in our direction.

This is where I decide once and for all that, after you are seated at a restaurant and it's been a while since any human being has made an attempt to contact you, it's preferable to be handed the menu rather than to be asked, 'What do yous fancy for yer tea?' I wonder what the tourists from Monterey make of it.

I'd also make a further point, carping as it is, carp carp carp, that if you enter a restaurant, ask for a table, then order wine, it's a teeny bit provocative to then be asked if you want to see the menu. I reflect that one of these nights when I'm tired and grizzly it'll probably be these words that will tip me over the edge.

'Could you tell me what the fish of the day is, please?'

A shrug. 'Not sure.'

'Could you find out?'

'Sure. JACKIE! JACKIE! What's the fish? TERAKIHI? ARE YOU SURE? It's terakihi.'

Yes, we gathered that, the tourists from Monterey ('What the hell's terrorkey Myra?') gathered that, people a mile away gathered that.

But outside it's raining and blowing a gale. Maybe things will improve . . . maybe you expect too much. Maybe the moon really is made of blue cheese.

'People rave about restaurants because other people are raving about them,' says my companion, to whom I raved about this restaurant. 'It's the old emperor-has-no-clothes principle,' she adds.

'Mmmn,' I say. Non-committal is best. This is not the time to remind her about that time she dragged me to the Glow Worm Café where we found that the name was a literal description of the speciality of the house. Yeah well, look, I'm as adventurous as the next one, but Crisped Worm Tortillas?

I study the menu. She studies the menu. Prawn cocktail. Prawn cocktail? Chicken and apricots. Chicken and apricots? What is this? Back to the 60s night? Where's the thyme chicken, the herbed fish, the pasta? Oh I see. A new chef. And he's a devotee of a new cuisine. Oh really?

'Well, there's been nouvelle cuisine, we've had Tex-Mex, Italian, Spanish, Worm, now there's a new one.'

'A new one?'

'Yes, the new one's called Post-Retro Retro. Really interesting food combinations. Tomato soup. Salad greens cut into fine ribbons and served with something he calls Highlander Mayonnaise. With sliced beetroot. You've noted the chicken and apricots. Porterhouse steak with crinkled chips. Oh, and I mustn't forget, something really cute. He serves these little round salty crackers with slices of tomato on them with your tea or coffee. Really taken on, they have.'

'I think I'll have steak.'

'Rare, medium?'

'Well done, please.'

'Well done?'

'That's what I said.'

'But no one orders steak well done.'

'I just have.'

'I dunno what the chef'll say.'

I no longer bother with a smile. 'No blood,' I say, 'no blood. Let me hear you say it out loud. *No Blood, No Blood.*'

'Okay,' she backs away, 'no need to get excited, no blood. I'll tell him.'

She disappears into the kitchen and the next minute she's back accompanied by a small thin man wearing a white singlet and blue and white striped trousers. He peers over at our table.

'NO BLOOD?' he mouths at me incredulously.

'FORGET IT,' I mouth back, giving him a V for Victory sign for good measure. I know when I'm beaten.

We pay for the wine, sing 'Pokarekare Ana' to the tourists from Monterey and promise to write. We drive to Happy Harriet's and buy fish and chips, to the bottle store for a heavenly Sauvignon Blanc and to the supermarket for a two-litre container of vanilla icecream and a packet of Mallowpuffs. We go home and everything's blissful.

Touring

I have travelled far and wide, wide and far around this country. I have toured with plays, with other writers, on my own. Compared to me, Michael Palin's a mere beginner, while Paul Theroux and Bill Bryson don't even know they're alive. I've been stuck in the lift in Waiouru Military Camp while my companions were living it up in the bar, locked in a lavatory on the Cook Strait ferry while my partner read her Georgette Heyer regardless (yes, I'm bitter and she's never heard the end of it), and left in a long drop in Greymouth while my colleagues sang and danced their way through the first half of a show before they realised I wasn't on stage with them.

I can't say I wasn't warned. Everyone I met told me touring was hell. But I knew better. They told me motherhood was hell but I knew better. I was going to be different. And I was. I have to hang on to that.

I mean, think about it. You take a van, jam six people in it with nothing in common but frustrated envy (everyone else has got better reviews), for eight hours each day. At various times you shove them out to talk and smile at strangers and then (as a treat for the writers, I presume) read some pages from their latest book. There is always a cup of tea and asparagus rolls which leave little bits of green stuff in everyone's teeth and are discovered only after the group has posed (smile, please!) for a photo for the local paper.

The driver of the van likes, nay adores, Glen Campbell or Janis Joplin and has brought every tape he could lay his hands on to help while away the hours. The driver of the van likes to sing along with either Glen or Janis. He specially likes to sing 'I am a Linesman for the County' or 'Hey, hey, hey, Bobby McGee, yuh'. He even sings it in the shower while the rest of us are having breakfast.

The only difference between touring the cast of a play and touring a group of writers is that the cast of a play know their lines (most of the time).

As you bump and swear your way over country roads where no Member of Parliament has ever driven, and skim smoothly along others which have received the care and attention necessary if an MP's tender bum is not to get calluses, you have a chance to think about life. You think about why you gave up teaching. You think about why you ever started writing. Most of all you wonder why the hell you ever said yes when that enthusiastic voice rang up and invited you on this goddamn tour.

And you smile. You smile at the people who wait for the van, you smile at people in petrol stations, you smile at your companions. You make a vow to yourself that when you get home you're not going to smile for a year. You discuss the motel (no flannels, TV wouldn't work, I swear a two-ton truck drove through the middle of my bedroom last night . . .). You don't discuss the fact that some of the group like to get up early, some like to get up late, some snore. You do not refer to the fact that some do early morning farts and pretend it's a car backfiring. You wish you were home, where what happens when you get up is a private matter.

In the van you review the reviewers — their sexual activities seem to come into it a lot — and you lead a group prayer that you will never ever see an asparagus roll ever ever ever again. This prayer is answered. In the negative. At the next stop.

The van is where you have a good grizzle to the only people in the world who will understand completely, who will laugh at the jokes you couldn't make anywhere else. It's also the place where emotions seethe. No need to go to Las Vegas for Fear and Loathing. At times it's so thick you can hardly see your way to your seat. It's so thick because the person who was asked to please keep to a ten-minute time limit, reads their bloody boring book right through, then confides at great length how they came to write it, what the difficulties were, and how many drafts they've put aside to sell to a university in the States when they hit the big time. They even tell you what the weather forecast was and how, as usual, it was wrong, ha ha.

Of course time ran out and there were only two minutes left for everyone else to read from their book and say how they came to write it. Insufferable. And what is worse, their book has been getting rave reviews. Not because their book is better, oh no, it's because they're a student of you-know-who, or the Books Editor owes them a favour, or their sister is married to the guy who works the lift for the Arts Minister. It's just not fair.

Touring solo is much the same, except there's no one to grizzle to. Sure, someone sees that you get to places on time and catch your plane, but she's not interested in listening to any worries. She has a husband who gambles, teenage kids who steal her running-away money to buy ecstasy (no, not that kind, the old-fashioned kind from the House of Pleasure), a sister who tells assembled relatives and guests at their parents' golden wedding that from now on she wants them to call her Harold. Her father is thrilled. He's always wanted a son called Harold. She always knew he liked her sister, uh, Harold, better than her. So why should she be interested in anything other than trundling you onto the plane on time, so she can go home and get stuck into the vodka?

I'm not talking first-class travel here. I'm talking little planes where the engine noise sets your eardrums quivering with agony so that you arrive with a blinding headache, unable to hear anything clearly for some days, let alone see your words on the page. Little planes where the sound system is so much a slave to static that the pilot could be screaming out *Jump, you fool* — could have already jumped, for all you know, and left you to drive the damned thing — when you think he's saying you'll be landing in five minutes.

Motels are the cheapest on offer and usually have elephants marching off to work past your door at 4.30 in the morning. These elephants may be the first talking pachyderms you've ever heard so you may be able to sell your story to television if it's a quiet week, but that is not much consolation at the time.

If the audiences are small, the organisers always tell you how they can't understand it, there were hundreds turned away for the last writer who came. And they expect you to smile as though you don't mind. Then they turn to you and say, 'How would you like to be introduced?'

As the ghost of Marilyn Monroe? Queen Salote? Winner of the Dominatrix of the Year Award? How about something about the books and plays I've written? Ugh, Ugh.

For some reason they expect you to be a good sport. Haven't they heard that writers are never good sports? If they were good sports they wouldn't be writers, they'd be flight attendants.

And you'll eat all the asparagus rolls, won't you, because asparagus gives the organiser indigestion.

Book signings. If you're very lucky, one person might turn up for the book signing, and if you talk in a lively animated fashion they might stay around for two hours so it doesn't look as though no one loves you. Or maybe they'll just think you've gone off your medication, and run like hell.

You always return home asking, Is there something wrong with me? Do I invite bad karma? If what goes round comes round, why do I keep getting incarcerated in lifts and lavatories? Is the big Travel Agent in the

Sky trying to tell me something? And your Significant Other always sighs deeply and reaches for the bottle opener.

Yes, touring is hell. There are the reunions, of course. These happen spontaneously when those of us who have stayed the course gather round the bar and relive some of the more desperate moments of the tours we shared. Like members of the Returned Services Association, we know that we are the only ones who will understand. No good trying to talk to family or friends, they will never comprehend what we went through.

Do you remember . . .

— The time the two in the next motel unit had a row in the middle of the night and he rushed outside screaming and threw her birth control pills on the roof?

— The time the van slipped on the snow and we nearly went over the cliff?

— The time we arrived at the hall and it was locked and not a soul in sight?

— The woman who stood up at question time and told the person chairing the meeting to leave her husband alone?

You had to be there.

Apostrophe's

Break out the Bolly, shovel out the smoked salmon, chuck on the caviar, I have launched myself into a new career. I have done my market research, I have identified a need and the results show there is a niche market just waiting for my kind of service.

Make way for the world's first Apostrophe Consultant. Your eye's are the first to be faced with these startling new revolutionary idea's, as set out below.

As well as offering consultancy on every aspect of apostrophe-using (Feeling the Fear but Using it Anyway) I will also hold Apostrophe Seminars for the academics among us (The Apostrophe in Apostrophe-Modernist World), and Workshopping Apostrophes (Apostrophes on Stage) for the arty-farty ones.

I'm not one of those experts who feels smug about her own far-reaching talent and skill, her ability to open up a new frontier of language or her comprehensive grasp of grammar and punctuation; no, I understand, indeed sympathise, with the prevailing confusion about apostrophe's. I too have had to struggle, to come to grips with apostrophe's in the 90's. It is no longer enough (source: letters written to papers by boring old farts or BOF's) to inform innocent children that there are only two occasions when you should use an apostrophe. You can demonstrate examples like 'cat's tail' or 'you mustn't' until you and the child are both blue in the face, the BOF's scream, but if you don't bring back the cane, make children stand in corners wearing placards that read I AM STUPID, and allow bullying in the playground, children will never learn about apostrophes.

The only trouble with the BOF theory is that the kids who were stood in corners, caned at least once a week and bullied daily when they were at school have trouble with apostrophe's too (source: look around you for Gods' sake, children are not writing the sign's in shops are they, Dumbo?).

There is another theory. This is put forward by people whose kids are encouraged from birth to be socially responsible or PWKAEFBTBSRs). Poor old apostrophe's, the PWKAEFBTBSRs cry (no scoffing, I'm working on empathetic imagination here), why should apostrophe's be confined to such pathetically meagre appearances when fullstops and commas are splashed about so liberally? Just because apostrophe's are in the minority, a small group in a strange country, why should they be discriminated against?

An imaginary conversation.

'I know, let's use an apostrophe whenever we feel like it, what do you reckon?'

'Hip ray hip ray!'

'Yay!'

'Wicked!'

'Choice!'

'Cool a's!'

One thing leads to another, and before you know where you are the kids who grew up with BOF's and the kids who are members of the PWKAEFBTBSRs group have joined forces and apostrophes are everywhere.

It has taken me years and a lot of screams of anguish (Did you see that? '*We develop your photo's in fifteen minute's!*') to get to this position, so believe me, I understand your reluctance. I really do. It is true that silly old pedantic me, the one that thought using an apostrophe was easier if you knew the rules and stuck to them, has gone. I am a new woman — but I have not forgotten what it felt like, dear. Although I can now gaze on strawberry's, blackberrie's, even raspberri's without a wince, a blench, or even a serie's of sigh's, my heart can still be wrung by a look of agony, a cry of anguish from some passer-by. I want to share this with you so that you know you are not alone.

My mission now is to get everyone in the Western world (for the moment, lets take it one day at a time ok, doesn't mean I don't have larger vision's, does it?) to forget the confusion's of the past, and concentrate on the future. The Year 2000 loom's. Don't get caught up in who'll be first to see the sun and temporary infatuation's of that nature. No, we must join together to make a better world by liberating apostrophes from their former constrictive prison — and what more significant time than the beginning of a new millennium?

Imagine a world where every apostrophe mattered. Imagine (yes I know John Lennon has got a lien on beginning sentences with this word; but, if you recall, he omitted to mention the power of apostrophe's to unite this sad old world — he plumped for love), a world where there were prizes (the 'Killing Two Bird's With One Stone' award) for the menu where

Souffle's of Kumara's (or Kumera's) appeared. Imagine the standing ovation for the sign advertising three tennis ball's for ten cent's.

Imagine a world where people cared enough about apostrophe's to encourage everyone to use some every day of their lives. If we are exhorted to eat five pieces of fruit per day so we will be healthier and live longer, why not extend the same criteria to apostrophe's? Yes, liberate apostrophe's, I say!

In any revolution there are those who lead the way, the ones far out front (BOF's and PWKAEFBTBSR's, I have no doubt), who go far far out so that the rest of us can take a few stumbling steps forward in perfect safety. I would not have the gall to claim affinity or kinship with social icons such as Mae ('Come up and see my apostrophe some time') West, Marilyn ('Apostrophes are a girl's best friend') Monroe or Muhammad ('Dance like a butterfly, sting like an apostrophe') Ali, but if I, in my small way, can follow in their footstep's, surely you can do the same.

You may be smiling. You may even be hissing and mocking. But wait. Think what the reaction was when Louis Armstrong first got up on stage to play his trumpet (who is this short black?), or when Boy George appeared and sang a first trembling note (who the hell is this flat white?) — and think how those critics were made to eat their words.

So, less of the curled lip when you see things like tomatoe's and pomme's de terre, not to mention this sign on an auto-electrician's window: *Try Our Tune-up's!*

This was slightly upstaged by another sign I saw on the same walk, advertising a play by Terence Rattigan called *Separate Table's*. This was when I knew that out there were those for whom my crie's had not fallen on deaf ear's, or been in vain. I was so overcome I had to have a little lie down.

Pass the Prozac and I'll get to work on my *Dictionary of Apostrophe Variables*. Sure to be a bestseller.

That's not Portland Island Lighthouse, darling, it's moi!

How would you like it if all of a sudden your face went geranium scarlet, your glasses steamed up, your body temperature shot up about 100 degrees, and something that felt like a million pimples suddenly decided to burst out and send their contents oozing all over your face and body?

I know, I know, I should have left you in blissful ignorance, I should have turned away as, like sheep trudging happily into the abattoirs, you continued on your journey towards the inevitable end. But I can't. Why should I be the only one to suffer?

What's that? You wouldn't mind if you had to rush madly to the door every half hour so you could fling it open and stand in the teeth of the lovely cold southerly, or delicious snow, hail, you name it, it doesn't matter as long as it's cold? You'd jump at carrying a roll of Handee paper towels in your bag when you go out; and you think it's nonsense to mind when a traffic cop pulls you over in the middle of rush-hour traffic because you look so red-faced and uncomfortable he thinks you're an escaped crim? Would you care if the store detective asked to search your bag just after you'd grabbed the display bottle and sprayed yourself with Passion all over in a frenzied attempt to get some sort of relief? Not you. You're made of sterner stuff. In any case, as you've made it perfectly clear to your hormones: it's all in the mind.

And what about the nights? The throwing off of bedclothes, the yells of anguish (*Why me? Why me?*), the tossing, the turning, the tears and gnashing of teeth. And that's just your Significant Other. *I'm sleeping with a menopausal woman! Aaaah!*

But hey, like people who drink and drive, people who have penetrative sex without condoms, those who think they'll never stop being prime minister, people like me Before the Change (BC), the menopause is never going to happen to you.

It's obvious, you sneer. If you expect so-called hot flushes then you'll have them. If you sit around worrying about things like nervous spasms, panic attacks, memory loss, loss of libido, osteoporosis, headaches, tiredness, sleeplessness, then obviously you're practically inviting them in. It's all in the mind. Even if you do score the occasional hot flush, hey, no need to make a song and dance about it. It's only feminists who do that, and you wouldn't want anyone to think you're a feminist, would you?

What has brought on this outburst of venom from one who is renowned for her calm and even temperament? What were the straws that broke the back of one who is known far and wide for waking up with a merry smile on her face? I suppose the following probably had something to do with it:

I really love my hot flushes (usually said with a girlish giggle). *They keep me lovely and warm in winter.* (I'd rather have sex, myself.)

Have you tried evening primrose capsules? (Yes. I think it was around the time I tried telling the waves to go back.)

My sister had hormone replacement therapy and she's fine now. (Your sister smiles all the time, too.)

I heard that it helps if you cut out fat. Or wheat. Or meat. Or cooked foods. (So it's not enough I have to endure these torments, you want my heart, liver and entrails as well?)

My homeopathist says you should cut down on tea and coffee and cut out alcohol completely. (I saw your homeopathist sneaking out of McDonald's last Friday night.)

You should try meditating, tai chi, yoga. (You should try a plaster across your mouth.)

Have you tried having sex morning and night? (Doesn't everybody?)

The next person to use the term 'hot flushes' to my face will be made to sit in a sauna, in their clothes, for five minutes every half hour for the rest of their life. At the same time they'll be expected to do their work, be nice to their colleagues, be pleasant to everyone on the phone and listen to idiots who offer meaningless soothing platitudes! And every time they break down in a sobbing heap asking *Why me?*, they'll be sent back to the sauna again for another dose. Get it?

Making the pizza

It's easy peasy to make pizza. All the books say so. I know this because I've read about a hundred books and they all say don't be frightened of working with yeast, making a pizza is easy. All you do, apparently, is stick some dried yeast on top of a little warm water with a snip of sugar, wait until it bubbles or froths, then shove it into some flour and a pinch of salt in a bowl or on a board, mix it all round with a little more water until it's soft and elastic, knead hell out of it for ten minutes then put it in a warm place for an hour or so. When it's doubled in size, give it a good punch, a few more kneads, then roll it out and slosh on the toppings. Shove in a hot oven and bake for twenty minutes or so and Bob's your auntie! Nothing to it.

Fired up with images of placing in the middle of the dining table a pizza that looks just like the photo on the cover of the hundredth cookbook, I write a list. Eventually (this must be what triathlon athletes do to train, so who am I to complain?) I find all the ingredients on the supermarket shelves, stagger home, line them all up on the bench and put my pinny on.

Warm water. How warm is warm? Is it hot warm or cold warm? And how the hell do you tell? I knew I should have got a cooking thermometer. I wonder, if I wrenched the built-in thermostat from the frozen turkey in the freezer would it work?

Better not.

I remember testing water for warmness in the days of bathing babies. You stuck your elbow in (the water, dummy, the water!) and if it was okay (what was okay? Shut up!) you lowered the screaming mouth into it. I tried sticking my elbow in the bowl of water waiting to receive the yeast, and slopped it all over the bench. Reason? My elbow was too big for the bowl. Not to worry. Get a bigger bowl. Problem solved.

You can hardly see the water in the bottom of my largest mixing bowl, but I know it's there because I felt it with my elbow and the temperature is bang on. Now, measure the yeast. This is not as easy as it sounds. I have three kinds of spoon measures — square, oblong and round. I like the round ones best. A Freudian would probably make a lot of that. But I don't care to discriminate, so I use the measures in turn. This time it's the turn of the oblong ones.

I measure the yeast. Doesn't look much — not enough to liven up four and a half cups of flour. I mean we're dealing with *live* organisms (go back and read the word again) here. Better see what the square one says. Still doesn't look enough. But it must be right. Better test the water again. The water's stone cold.

Get more warm water, test, quickly scatter yeast over top before it cools. Add the sugar. Stand and watch. Stand and watch? Well of course I stand and watch. If I don't it might froth when I'm not looking, and then what will happen?

Finally there seems to be some sort of movement down there in the bowl. A heaving of the waters, you might say. And lo, there is froth. Shit, there's froth! I mean it's really froth! Hey, look! It's frothing! My God, it's *frothing*! What do I do now? Where's the book? Where's the bloody book?

Under the bowl. Right. I knew that.

How much flour? Four and a half cups. I have three kinds of cup measures, round, oblong and square, but I'm not buggering around any longer. I'll use the round one and to hell with it. Doesn't look much. Doesn't look like four and a half cups on the baking board. Well it is, so get on with it.

Make a well in the centre. How deep a well? Don't start that. And how do I make a well in the centre of a mound of flour and *at the same time* stop flour spraying off the board onto the bench, the floor, the stove top, the cat, me? At the rate I'm going there'll be no flour left to make a well in. Quickly, before you lose any more, put the frothy mixture in the middle of the well and add the rest of the warm water from the second largest bowl where it's just been tested, okay?

Bad move. As well as flour, water is now dribbling onto the bench, the floor, the stove top, the cat and me. Well, don't just stand there telling Jesus all about it, you fool, start mixing!

There won't be enough frothy stuff because most of it is on the floor being licked up by the dog. Don't panic. Just mix it all, or what's left of it, together. Don't worry about the yeast frothing inside the dog. Remember, she ate three rusty screws which fell out of the arch holding up the Birthday Present Rose, and followed that with a munch on a couple of metres of garden twine — and never turned a hair. Dogs have a very simple digestive system and hers will cope with the odd bit of yeast, okay?

There are now two kinds of mixtures on the board. One lot is a hard little knob composed of flour and frothy stuff and the other is the pathetic remnant of flour which has remained on the board. Like a group of Christian fundamentalists faced with a bunch of Queer activists, there is no common ground. Making an executive decision, I throw some water *straight from the tap* onto the board and hey presto, a ball seems to be forming.

Now. Kneading. I know how to knead. I saw Alison Holst do it on television years ago. You just push the left side of the dough on top of itself with the heel of your left hand, then push it back to base with the heel of your right hand. And you keep this up until the hard unyielding ball becomes soft, pliant and elastic. Sounds a little bit like a Mills & Boon, but you get the drift.

So I start. And I'm lucky. National Radio, which recently concluded the riveting thirteen-part series *Mosquitoes of the Andes*, has cassettes available which I can get by sending a cheque to their postbox. But that's not why I'm lucky, although I wouldn't want to knock the devotees who jump into the air and yell yippee at the thought of owning a tape of *Mosquitoes of the Andes*. Especially as National Radio is throwing in a free cassette of *Manuel of the Mountains* to those fortunates whose cheques are among the first 1000 to be opened.

No, I'm lucky because National Radio has today just begun broadcasting a new thirty-part series which features pop singers of the past. In fact it's called *Pop Singers of the Past*.

This would not be all that interesting in a reflection on pizza-making were it not for the fact that the first featured pop singer from the past is someone this expert from the past has never heard of. Wee Wallie Winkie. *Wee Wallie Winkie?* Oh well, you never know what's hiding in National Radio archives, do you? I take a deep breath and begin kneading. And what do you know, Wee Wallie launches into a song which must have been written to aid the kneading of pizza dough. Good old National Radio, eh?

Well-a-rock-rock-rock, and-a-roll-roll-roll
I've got a funny *feel*ing in my soul soul *soul*

Before I know where I am (in a flour and yeast-spattered kitchen) the dough is kneaded, put into an oiled bowl, covered with plastic and placed on top of some towels in the hotwater cupboard.

Oh goody! An hour which I can use to clean the kitchen from top to toe.

The hour up, the kitchen shining as it has never shone before, I repair to the hotwater cupboard. I open the door. Aaah! The dough has broken out of its prison of glass and plastic and has not only risen over the towels, but, like an avalanche, has covered everything in its path.

Two hours or so (three washing-machine loads and a complete spring-clean of the hotwater cupboard) later, I capture the last of the pizza dough, wrap it in six sheets of newspaper and thrust it into the rubbish bag, where it rumbles away to itself. *Die!* I yell, and without a qualm, tie up the top of the rubbish bag and put it out the front for the rubbish collectors.

I make a vow to turn my attention to making something easier. Mille-feuille, perhaps.

Oh yes, we had pizza for tea that night. It looked just like one of the stunning photos in the pizza cookbooks. It's amazing what you can find at a supermarket when you're looking for pizza makings.

On hearing poems read in a pub one Thursday night

I walk the lonely streets
Nobody knows my name
Thank God.
Tonight I was dragged along to a pub
I hate pubs
I hate pubs because
Noisy people go there.
I hate pubs because everyone smokes
I mean they like, *smoke*, man.
The grey smoke rises above the heads of the noisy people
As they go to the bar and order a Steinie or even a Steiny.
I hate pubs because they stink of booze
And piss
And other things like shit, vomit, mince, rotten fish.
But most of all I hate pubs because
People read poems there.
Tonight a man read a poem
About loss — he'd lost his wife apparently
Somewhere between the main street and the railway station.
She just vanished.
And now he's alone
On his own
And he's having a moan
And sometimes a groan
O please, my darling
Please come home.
I stood up.
I said
If I was her
I'd have left you long ago
You're nothing

But
A Moaning Mickey
A whinger
And you really should take your hands off it.
He chased me out of the pub
But I ran faster
It's funny how fast you run
When you're being chased by a man
With a sheaf of poems in his hand
That he wants to read to you
So you'll understand.
I walk the lonely streets
Nobody knows my name
Thank God
They won't be able to ring me up
And read poems over the phone.

Pigeon or pear?

Apart from Stick Insects, the world of female humans is divided into two distinct shapes. Pigeon or Pear. Pigeons have heavy top halves; Pears have heavy bottom halves. Put bluntly, this means that Pigeons have Big Boobs and Pears have Big Bums.

I am a female Pigeon and I have a few grizzles I've been saving up. Like all passionate protesters wanting to right the wrongs of the world, I only care about the things that affect me me me, so I'm going to concentrate on the disadvantages of being a Pigeon. If the Pears want to do anything about righting the world for them, they can get off their big bums and do it themselves.

Female Pigeons have big chests. Pigeons pay a lot more for bras, shirts and jackets. Bras increase in price according to the size of the proposed wearer. This is unfair, unjust and downright unkind. Is it the fault of a female Pigeon if she has big breasts? No, it is not. Big or small breasts come at the whim of a Pigeon's gene pool. Why should she be penalised simply because her mother and grandmother had big breasts? When you think about it, it's the same principle as charging for tampons and sanitary pads.

Not that I'm suggesting for one moment that we women *mind* paying for tampons and pads, whether we want to or not. No, no, periods are a luxury and we're very lucky to have the privilege of feeling rotten one week out of four. If we start menstruating at thirteen and stop at fifty, that's thirty-seven years, which means we all live in happy anticipation of 444 weeks of bliss. No wonder some of us get pregnant. Of course there are some who start at twelve and finish at fifty-one, and these jackpot winners are looking at 468 times of wonder. How do any of us contain our rapture at the thought of it? How lucky can you get? Think of all that lovely money we could fritter away on holidays, clothes, wine and, of course, superannuation investments — all spent wisely on tampons and pads. That's why mothers, grandmothers, sisters, cousins, aunties, friends or neighbours can be seen any day of the week dancing in supermarket aisles waving packets of tampons and pads and screaming, *Yippee, I'm getting my period tomorrow, let's celebrate!*

But I digress.

A Pigeon has a bad time when she's trying on clothes. If the skirt or trousers from a suit fit, the top looks like a bolero. If you breathe in and hold it for the count of fifty while you force the buttonholes over the buttons, they pop off all over the fitting-room floor and you have to hide the top underneath all the other tops with buttons missing. If the top fits, you can usually get the shop assistant into the trousers or skirt as well. As for anything remotely like a bikini, forget it. Well, if you're a true Pigeon you probably forgot it at around age twelve.

But, you cry, *these days there are racks of tops and racks of trousers and you can make up your own suit.* Of course there are, but sometimes the Pigeon likes something a bit more upmarket, okay? Is that a crime? To want to look stylish? To wear a designer suit occasionally? Uh? Uh?

Pigeons always have problems with trousers. They are always too long or too short. That is because, for some genetic reason (for those who believe in God, blame feminism; for those who don't, blame God or Ms Darwin), Pigeons are never medium height, they're either quite tall or quite short. Therefore, trousers made to fit the average leg never work for Pigeons. Pigeons always find that all the trousers in the entire ten shops they've been to that day are about a metre too long or a metre too short — and Pigeons are never any damn good at taking up hems. All those females you see lying on the floors of shops drumming their heels and bawling *I hate shopping* are Pigeons.

Yes, you could go down the racks and try and nick a pair of trousers from a size 12 suit to go with the jacket from a size 16 but if the Stick Insect assistant catches you there'll be hell to pay. The only hope you've got is to search for a shop where there's one assistant who is a Pigeon. They're few and far between, but there are some. She will turn a blind eye while you mix and match the 12s and 16s. The only trouble is that, with your luck, every other Pigeon in the world will have been there before you, leaving in their wake hundreds of size 12 jackets and size 16 trousers and skirts. But hey, at the very least you can both have a tantrum together.

Pigeons never wear jerseys unless they're (a) crazy, (b) hyperventilating because they're freezing, or (c) have access to huge shapeless fishermen's-knit sacks or the occasional Fair Isle which a Pear friend (?) has given them because it's been washed the wrong way and has drooped. If Pigeons have a rush of blood to the head and force one of those cute little elasticised tops with scoop necklines over their head, they find it fits properly over only one boob. The other either gets squeezed under their armpit or jammed under the belt of their trousers (if you have been a nursing mother this is the more likely possibility), and this makes sitting and walking extremely uncomfortable.

T-shirts stocked by menswear shops have a lot going for them. For a start, the ones labelled large are *too big*. Unbelievable. You *have* to buy a medium unless you want to go somewhere formal and need a T-shirt with a train. It's so long since you bought a medium anything you have to keep taking the T-shirt off and showing the label to friends, relatives, people in the street. See? See? Medium!

There are a lot of Pigeons around and you'd think manufacturers would have tumbled to this, but no, they keep doggedly churning out thousands of 8s and 10s. So that they won't be seen as lacking in compassion and consideration for the seriously obese, they might throw in oh, say, ten size 12s and five size 14s. Every Pigeon who has ever gone into a shop and been faced with racks and racks of 8s and 10s and been told that the 12s and 14s went in the first five minutes feels very grateful for their kindness, I'm sure.

The really ugly scenes are when two Pigeons stumble on the same suit (size 16 jacket, size 12 pants made for the manufacturer's lover but she didn't like the colour) at exactly the same moment, and both think they were first. The drive and determination to win displayed by both sides when the All Blacks play South Africa for the World Cup is nothing compared to that displayed by two Pigeons wanting the same suit. Eye-gouging, head-high tackling, forward passing, running on the blind, deliberate tripping, you name it, it's all there. There can only be one outcome. That mangled wreck on the floor is the suit. But the Pigeons are happy. At least *she* didn't get it. They shake hands and walk out smiling.

However, I have a solution to this perennial problem. I suggest that Pigeons strike up a close relationship with Pears. So simple. But so is the theory of relativity when you boil it down. Think about it — world peace may depend on getting this right. Imagine (yes I know I've used this before) a world where Pigeons and Pears shopped for suits together. Imagine a world where Pigeons and Pears got together. Imagine . . . but that's enough. You get my drift.

NEW YEAR'S REVOLUTIONS I

I will be invited to do the performance reviews of any public relations administrators in the health system who earn over $80,000. If their job is to make me believe that waiting lists have grown because more people are getting sicker and not because the health system has been deliberately run down over the last ten years, they have failed, dismally. If their job is to make me believe that what the Minister for Health says is the truth, then they've failed. If their job is to make me think everything's fabulous in the health system, it's just that I'm so thick I don't understand it, then they've failed. Two weeks' notice and no, repeat *no* bonus, that's what I say.

Whoever chooses Queen Elizabeth's clothes will be forced to wear her cast-offs for the next ten years.

Whoever chooses Queen Elizabeth's hats will be charged with grievous bodily harm to a monarch.

Bill Clinton and Saddam Hussein will be locked in a room in Queenstown and told they won't be allowed out until they kiss and make up. Just a friendly kiss, nothing too intense.

All students will leave school at age twelve, spend the next five years learning and working in some practical discipline like professional theatre, film, ballet, music, sport, gardening, and then five years in some more ephemeral area such as business administration, accountancy, finance. Then, those who wish to may attend university and study towards degrees in science, physics, humanities, medicine, geology, geography, zoology, horticulture et al. All right, it's a dream, but hey — when reality's not working, that's all you've got left, isn't it?

All those over seventy will be awarded a red convertible sports car or a year in Italy studying opera or cooking, their choice.

What did he mean to you?

'Good afternoon, listeners. Here is the news, read by Aubrey Blickett, on this first Thursday after Christmas. Of course there's no real news because the politicians have all gone to ground and as I speak are stuffing themselves silly with grog and turkeys paid for by the ordinary taxpayer who has had to manage with a chicken on special from the supermarket washed down with a bottle of sparkling wine which they bought at discount for $4.95. There have been no car accidents unfortunately, no murders, no domestic violence, but we will do our best with what we have to hand.

'There was a special sitting at the High Court in Wellington today when a man, accused of deliberately driving a bull into a china shop on Christmas Eve and causing $500,000 worth of damage, appeared before Judge Jarrod Jinkelberry. Here's our court reporter Francine Sparrows-Hoop Brown *live* from the courthouse, to report on this enthralling case which has gripped the nation over the last three days. Well, as I say, there's been precious little else happening. Good afternoon Francine.'

'Good afternoon Aubrey. The police prosecutor, Tremaine Clarke, alleges that the accused deliberately led his pet bull into a china shop, knowing full well the effect this would have on the bull. Clarke said that the proprietor of the china shop had recently ended her five-year relationship with the accused, and the accused was seeking revenge. As you and the listeners will know, Aubrey, bulls and china shops are a fatal mix.'

'A fatal mix, Francine, yes.'

'The accused, whose name has been suppressed to protect his cousin, Deemon Conks, who lives in Epsom, Auckland, Epsom Avenue I believe, that big house on the corner, two-storey, large trees, you know the one I mean, Aubrey? '

'Has it got two big oak trees by the front gate, Francine?'

'I think it has, Aubrey, yes.'

'With Christmas lights hanging all over them?'

'That's the one, Aubrey.'

'Well I don't suppose there could be two properties like that, could there, Francine?'

'Unlikely, Aubrey.'

'And what did the accused have to say, Francine?'

'He said that what happened was exactly the opposite of what the police alleged. He reckons that he was walking along the footpath with his pet bull when the animal — maddened with lust, the accused suggests, on catching sight of a china bull in the window — went berserk. It charged into the shop like a bull at a gate, the accused says, dragged the accused into the shop and attempted to mate with the china bull. Any damage done happened when the accused was trying to drag the bull out of the shop. He said that the proprietor was no help, and only added to the damage by screaming obscenities and flailing around with a china lampstand, which enraged the bull even further — not to mention the accused. The accused said he had to have three stitches on his arm, and the bull, which was very distressed, had to be given a calming injection so it could be moved from the shop in the vet's stationwagon, and if anyone should have brought charges it was him, not the shop proprietor.

'When questioned by Judge Jarrod Jinkelberry as to why he was walking a bull along a public footpath anywhere near a china shop when everyone knew bulls shouldn't be allowed within a bull's roar of one, the man said he had walked his pet bull along that footpath for five years and there had never been any incidents previously.

'The judge adjourned the case until tomorrow. I asked Police Prosecutor Tremaine Clarke whether he was happy with the progress of this case, which has attracted big headlines in the national newspapers for the last two days.'

Tremaine: I'm afraid I can't comment on any aspect of the trial but I think I *can* say we are *pleased* with the *progress*.

Francine: You're *pleased* with the *progress*?

Tremaine: I think, yes, I think I can say that.

Francine: Thank you.

'That was Police Prosecutor Tremaine Clarke outside the High Court in Wellington, commenting on the progress of the trial which has gripped the nation for the last three days. This is Francine Sparrows-Hoop Brown reporting from the High Court in Wellington. Over to you, Aubrey.'

'Thank you, Francine. That was our court reporter Francine Sparrows-Hoop Brown reporting *live* from the High Court in Wellington. We invited the Minister of Justice to comment, but he declined.

'Now to our next enthralling news item. Today a man fell fifteen stories after drinking a bottle of whisky, two bottles of milk and 50 mls of lemon juice. Jock Strapp has two broken legs, a broken arm, a dislocated shoulder, two black eyes, a broken nose, a broken jaw and three badly bruised ribs. Francine Sparrows-Hoop Brown interviewed him at the hospital.'

Francine: How are you feeling, Mr Strapp?

Jock: My cold's a hell of a lot better. My old grannie always said whisky, milk and lemon would do the trick.

Francine: Thank you Mr Strapp.

'That was Francine Sparrows-Hoop Brown reporting from the bedside of Jock Strapp, who had a bad fall today. And to those people ringing in complaining about the news content, may I just point out we at National Radio can hardly manufacture a gang killing or a car accident just to satisfy your craving for murder and violence, can we? Those kind of tactics might suit those who loll around on commercial radio, but here at National Radio we have ethics — we don't stoop to tacky means to drum up the ratings. I'm sorry, but there it is. Now . . .

'A woman accused of using her house as a brothel claims she is just a friendly soul who likes to help people and that this has been misunderstood. When asked why, when the police raided the house, a woman and a sailor were found in a compromising position in every room, she replied that the women were members of the local amateur repertory theatre group rehearsing *Hello Sailor*, and they wanted to hear first-hand how sailors cope with homesickness and other side effects of being away from home. Our court reporter Francine Sparrows-Hoop Brown was unable to be in court for this trial, due to another engagement, but we understand the trial continues tomorrow. Again we asked the Minister of Justice to comment, but again he declined.

'At the Auckland airport today, the woman whose husband left her to follow the Spice Girls around the world says she is devastated. Here's Francine Sparrow-Hoop Brown *live* at the airport.'

Francine: I understand you and your husband were together for twenty years.

Woman: That's right, twenty years, yes.

Francine: That's a long time.

Woman: A long time, yes.

Francine: What did he mean to you?

Woman: He meant everything to me, yes.

Francine: I understand you have just celebrated your twentieth wedding anniversary?

Woman: Our twentieth, yes.

Francine: So how do you feel, knowing he's left you for the Spice Girls?

Woman: Devastated. I feel devastated, yes.

Francine: You feel devastated?

Woman: Very bad, yes, very bad, yes.

Francine: What did he mean to you?

Woman: He meant everything to me, yes.

Francine: And you're devastated.

Woman: That's right, yes.

Francine: You said, I think, that your husband meant everything to you?

Woman: He meant everything to me, yes.

Francine: I don't want to put words in your mouth, but are you saying you were very close?

Woman: We were very close yes, and he meant everything to me.

Francine: Thank you.

'This is Francine Sparrows-Hoop Brown reporting from the airport.'

'Thank you Francine, you dragged that one out beautifully. That was Francine Sparrows-Hoop Brown live from the airport, and that concludes this news bulletin. As I said, I'm very sorry about the content but there's nothing we can do in the national newsroom if Members of Parliament go on holiday, and people refuse to drink and drive, hit their wives or kill each other. If you have any further complaints please write to the Minister of Broadcasting, maybe he can get the Minister of Justice to comment. This is Aubrey Blickett for National Radio.'

Dear Publisher

Dear Publisher,

I wish to apply for an advance to enable me to write a novel. I haven't started it yet but I read the book which won the 1997 Brilliant Book Awards and I know I can do just as well.

My life has been filled with crisis and drama, twists and turns of fate, so I feel a book based on my life would be very successful. It's not just me thinking this. Many times my friends have said, why don't you write a book Liz, instead of talking about it.

Here, so you'll get the idea, are a few highlights from my life.

HIGHLIGHTS FROM MY LIFE

I'm the second oldest of five girls. Our parents had very little money. My father inherited this place when his uncle died and we all knew that when my father died it would go to a cousin, so it was up to us to do what we could for ourselves. My older sister, Janie, was a nice girl, everyone said so, but my three younger sisters were real bad news. The two youngest, Kitty and Lydia, were absolute dillbrains — after anything in trousers (sorry to be crude but that's how it was) — and the next one, Mary, was an A-plus pain in the arse (sorry!) who was always reading the Bible and maundering on about God and duty and that. Not that I'm knocking people who believe in that sort of thing, but a little goes a long way, I'm sure you agree.

One day a rich young man, Bingo, came to live in the same village and he and Jane took a shine to each other. His sisters and his best mate weren't so keen on us. I have to admit when my Mum gets wound up she does talk a bit loud and my father always has his head in a book but nobody's perfect are they and as I always say you can choose your friends but not your relations ha ha. Bingo's best mate was called Darce, a bit poncy I know, but some parents never think, do they? The word was he had a big property down south, been in the family for generations, apparently. Some people have all the luck, eh. Darce was really up himself, thought his shit didn't stink to be honest. Looked at us as though we were something the cat dragged in, wouldn't talk, wouldn't dance, wouldn't mix at all. To be quite frank we didn't hit it off at all. So when he wandered up and asked me for a dance I said, 'Get your hand off it, mate!'

Things went from bad to worse. Bingo's sisters and Darce worked on the guy and he left the district and my sister high and dry. Meanwhile Lydia and Kitty were making fools of themselves with some soldiers who were camping in the district, doing military exercises. My sisters were making real idiots of themselves. Although I must admit they didn't have to try very hard. I talked to Mum and Dad about it but it was like talking to a brick wall.

Anyway, the upshot was that Lydia, when she was away for a holiday with the colonel's wife, ran off with this guy called Wick for short. Well named, as it turned out. Everyone, including me, thought he was the cat's pyjamas, but it turned out that he was a stinko of the first water.

But I'm getting ahead of myself. I was staying at my cuzzie's (a nerd but his wife was a friend of mine), when who should appear but Darce. He got all white and trembly, said he shouldn't be doing what he was doing, I was from a fairly dicey family, but he couldn't help himself — and then he popped the question! Talk about flabbergasted. I was speechless. But only for a second. I wasn't going to have some wanker like Darce slagging off my family. I mean, for me to do it is one thing, but he hardly knew them! Well, the long and short of it was that I told him to shove his hook. He didn't like that one little bit. Especially when I told him I'd seen better manners on dead hedgehogs and a few other things, one of them being about his treatment of Wickie. I got right up his nose, so much so that he wrote me a letter.

You could have knocked me down with a feather. What a turn-up. It looked as though Wickie had led us all right up the garden path. Not to put too fine a point on it, he and the truth had a fairly distant relationship. After reading Darce's letter I didn't feel too good about some of the things I'd said to the poor bugger, but there was nothing I could do because he'd taken himself off. I'd really put my foot in it and (not for the first time) I said to myself, 'You've really done it this time, Lizzie, my girl.'

To cheer myself up I went off on holiday to the South Island with my auntie and uncle. She was keen to go on some garden tours which she'd seen advertised. I hadn't wanted to go on this tour because one of the houses was Darce's, but my auntie's mad on gardens and someone said the family was away, so I thought, why not? Might as well admit that when I saw the place I thought, well, well well, you certainly gave yourself the short straw here, Liz my girl. Then, as I was turning round a corner, surprise surprise, who should be walking up the path but Darce! He was a bit subdued at first, and to tell you the truth I wasn't my usual self. Talk about awkward. I did the intros and he was very nice to my auntie and uncle. Asked us to meet his sister, and said, what about a bite to eat sometime?

We were getting along good-oh, and just as I started to think well, maybe . . . I got a letter from Janie to say that Lydia had run off with Wickie! I was gobsmacked, I don't mind admitting it. I always knew Lydia was stupid, but.

Anyway, that spelt the end of any hopes I might have had that me and Darce would ever get together. Talk about down. It's no exaggeration to say that my bottom lip was dragging on the ground. I mean, if Darce thought my family was pretty dire before what would he think now? And who could blame him? Certainly not yours truly.

But it just shows. You should never think every door is closed. Just when I thought that life with a capital L was over for me, things took a turn for the better. Wickie actually married Lydia and got a job up north, and when he and Lydia called in for the weekend on their way up there, Lydia let it slip that Darce had organised it all. The wedding, the job, everything. Even paid Wickie's bills! You wouldn't believe it, would you.

Then Bingo turned up and started making up to Janie again. Then they got engaged. My Mum was in seventh heaven. Darce was around a bit when Bingley first came back, then he disappeared before I could even thank him. The next thing, Darce's old drag of an auntie called in and had a go at me. Wanted me to promise I'd never marry her nephew because he was promised to her daughter. 'Does Darce know about this?' I asked, and you should've seen the old devil's face. I thought she was going to have a fit. In the end she flounced off making all sorts of threats, but hey, some people are like that, aren't they? Can't get their own way, they make everyone's life a misery. Or try to.

Yeah, you can see a happy ending coming up, can't you? And you'd be right. Darce appeared the next day and we had a talk, got things straightened out. We'd both been up ourselves, we admitted, and we were both sorry. The long and short of it is that we got married, a double wedding with Janie and Bingo. A real nice do, that was.

That's as far as I want to take the story of my life at this stage. If you could see your way clear to advancing me some money I'd be very grateful.

A cash cheque would be best. You see I want to keep it a surprise from Darce. I'm looking forward to seeing his face when I present him with the finished book. I know he'll be really chuffed. And I'm sure you can see the huge film potential.

I remain,
Yours faithfully,

Liz Darcy.

GARDENING WITH RENÉE II

Other people bore on and on about their garden. You wonder why they don't notice that they're being boring. It is so fatally easy to become boring, you think; and you reflect that boring people never notice they're being boring, otherwise they wouldn't be boring, would they? In the meantime, just to liven things up, you'll tell them about the strange and wonderful things that have happened to the ten-year-old Heritage rose you surrounded with sheep pellets last month, and then go on to tell them the really hilarious things your grandchildren said about the sheep pellets; then, if the atmosphere is still a bit dead, you'll make them smile by telling them all about your new puppy's (rather gross but we've finished eating haven't we?) predilection for sheep pellets.

If someone says deprecatingly (only way to say it!) that their garden's a tip, don't, repeat *do not* look around at their weed-strewn, disease-ridden, rusting-car-laden mess of a section, laugh gaily (all right!) and say, you're right there, all you need are the plastic bags and the seagulls, ha ha.

When someone complains about their garden soil being poor and says they can't understand it, and you know they bought just the one bag of compost to go round their half-acre paradise, don't say a word. No no, not a word! Not one! *Not!* Oh well.

When you buy five packets of seeds from a famous-writer's-birthplace shop (twice) and the only ones that appear above the surface of the ground are the ones whose packet with their name on has been lost, you could try writing about it.

The day Ernie nearly lost his wife

(from a collection found in an old exercise book)

Sunday started off not a bad sort of day as days go. Wind a bit strong. Thought we were going to part company with the roof at one stage but all that happened was that three trees and some telegraph poles were blown down. We've had worse. Still, bit too much wind to mow the lawns. A bit of a nuisance really. Sunday's the only day I get.

Well, old Ernie came ambling up the drive. I said, hello Ernie, and he said, hello Tom, and then he asked if he could use the phone. Mrs Ernie cuts off the phone each year when Ernie's finished at the Works for the season. The wife says she doesn't save anything really because it costs just as much to get it put back on, but I says, well, Reet, it takes all sorts. She says, well, she needn't think she can come in here every five minutes and use our phone, so there.

This Sunday Reet was off taking her Mum to church, and I'm not one of these types that mind helping out your neighbour, so I said, yeah, okay Ernie, come on in. We passed the time of day as neighbours do. Ernie and I don't see a lot of each other, he being off work until the next season starts, and me doing shift, so we took the time to catch up.

Ernie said he'd dug his ground over ready for the spuds in the spring and I said I'd just been told about a new green pea that was all the rage in Australia apparently. Ernie says his boy reckons he's mad growing his own spuds, cheaper in the supermarket when you work out the cost of labour and seed potatoes, but Ernie says he's been growing his own spuds for the last forty years and it's a bit late to stop now.

Ernie nodded at the phone and I got him the telephone book but he just waved it away. I heard him dialling, just the three numbers. And then he said, fire service please. I pricked up my ears at that. Fire service? Then I heard him say, I wish to report a fire.

I didn't wait to hear the rest. I dashed outside and sure enough, there was smoke coming from the back of Ernie's place. Shit, I thought. I put on a bit of a spurt, grabbed the hose and dragged it over to the fence. Shit,

I thought again. Some kids ran up the path and got up on the roof of our garage to have a better look. Some other neighbours tore along the grass verge and stood staring. Shit, I heard one of them say.

Next thing Ernie joins me on the path. He looks at the smoke and shakes his head. Wife's gonna go crook, he says, she's been at me not to burn the dog's bones on the stove. He looked at the smoke again. It's the fat, he says, gotta get rid of the fat somehow, otherwise you got flies. He shook his head. Doesn't look too good, he said, and went down our path.

Doesn't look too good, one of the neighbours said, as Ernie passed.

Just then I heard the fire engine siren and the red machine came careering round the corner of the street, firemen clinging to it on all sides. It's still a volunteer fire brigade round here and some of the guys had left home in such a hurry they were still doing up their trousers.

Two of them tore inside and we heard some crashing as they got to work with their axes. Another couple lugged the big hose inside and there was the sound of gushing. We shook our heads at each other. I knew we were all thinking the same thing: gonna be a bit of a mess. Mrs Ernie's not gonna be too thrilled, I thought. Two of the back windows suddenly smashed outwards and a fireman's face in a helmet looked out.

Then along the footpath comes Mrs Ernie. She'd been to church. She's a Mickey Doo and goes off to mass at least once on a Sunday. Well, Mrs Ernie takes one look at the fire engine and then gallops inside. I hear her screaming from where I'm standing. They probably heard her at the church, which was about a block away.

Told you not to put fat on the fire, she's yelling. Then there was a godalmighty screech and Ernie runs out carrying his missus. I think I've lost the wife! he calls, what have I done, that's all I want to know, what have I done? To tell you the truth he was panicking a bit.

Thank God, I thought, when I saw Reet tearing up Ernie's drive. She grabs Mrs Ernie, lays her on the front lawn, and starts mouth to mouth. Through a clean hankie, of course. Reet always carries a clean hankie since she went to that St John's First Aid Course they had at CWI last winter. We all gather round. Mrs Ernie's face was a sort of cold grey colour and one of the other neighbours rushed inside and got a blanket and spread it over her. Poor old Reet must've been just about giving up when finally Mrs Ernie's eyelashes start to flutter. She'll do, gasped Reet, but you'd better watch yourself Ernie. You were lucky this time, next time you might lose her.

They couldn't save the back of the house, unfortunately, but as we all said, things could've been worse. I mean the whole lot could've gone. There was a moment or two there when I even thought the flames might leap the fence over to my place. Yeah, we were all lucky. Sorry about the phone, I says to Reet, but seeing it was an emergency I thought I'd better let him use it. Reet just gives me one of her looks. She's a dag, is Reet.

Still, have to admit that the day Ernie nearly lost his wife made a bit of an impact on the neighbourhood. It's heading to go down in local history, the way these things do, and on the way gathering a few extras, if you get my drift. So I thought I'd write down the facts before the embroidery gets too fancy. So this is it. The true story of the day Ernie nearly lost his wife.

When I'm grown up

When I was a kid and under the thumb of any passing adult I used to promise myself that life would be better when I was grown up. I thought this would probably be when I was about thirteen. While I waited I spent a lot of time dreaming of all the glorious treats in store.

I spent a lot of time dreaming anyway, or with my head in a book, two activities frowned on by Mum. You'll go blind, she warned me, every time she caught me reading by the light of a stolen candle gummed to a saucer. Poor Mum, she didn't realise there was another activity which was also alleged to lead to this. Not that it matters. She was wrong about that as well. In any case my being hooked on reading was all her fault. She'd taught me to read in a desperate (and unsuccessful) bid to stop me talking.

I took to reading like a dehydrated dog to water and still managed to fit in a bout or two of questions about life. You know the kind of thing. Who am I? Why am I here? Why was Mr Smith from next door lying on top of Mrs Jackson from over the road, in the lupins at the river? Mum? Just your ordinary everyday questions. Mum's life was littered with these small daily challenges.

As for dreaming, I was born doing it apparently. That child is a dreamer, the nurse said, as she smacked me on the bum for the third time because I wasn't screaming my head off after the first belt. That was my first intimation that this old world wasn't really geared up for dreamers. I like to think I got my own back on the old cow by shitting all down the front of her nice white smock, but maybe it was just another lie adults tell kids when they want to convince them that every other adult in the world except them is an untrustworthy ningnong, so your best bet is to stick to what this particular adult is telling you. Only they have your best interests at heart. So work hard and don't ever dye your hair or wear short skirts.

I dreamed what it would be like when I dug under the old apple tree and found the trunk of old gold coins which had been put there by a man who'd stolen it from another man who'd found gold in Gabriel's Gully.

I dreamed what it would be like when I woke up with long thick curly golden hair instead of thin lank short brown.

I dreamed what it would be like to be so clever that I knew everything and I'd never have to go to school.

I dreamed what it would be like to have a shining long pink dress like my auntie's which I would wear all the time and not just to balls.

I dreamed what it would be like to live in a flash two-storey house like the doctor's kids did.

I dreamed about what would have happened if it had been Mrs Smith who discovered Mr Smith and Mrs Jackson in the lupins. This was the only one out of three million dreams which came true. Someone sent Mrs Smith a registered letter and told her about Mr Smith and Mrs Jackson. I was sitting at the front window staring into space, as Mum termed my dreaming ('People will think you're a sandwich short if you're not careful!'), when I saw Mrs Smith chasing Mr Smith down the road with the axe she must have grabbed from its place on their wood block, as she passed.

Mr Smith was holding up his trousers and running like Api Pene who won all the big boys' races at school and at the Labour Day Sports. I ran after Mrs Smith. I had been dreaming about what would happen when the teachers discovered I was a natural genius and made me the dux in Standard Two, but this was better. She chased him down past the corner shops, past the chemist's and the fruit and veggie shop, and everyone came out and watched. Mr Smith only escaped Mrs Smith and the axe by jumping over the Post Office counter and locking himself in the cupboard where Miss Beach, the postmistress, kept the registered mail. Mrs Smith cleared the counter after him and was all set to take to the door with the axe but Miss Beach said, although she sided with Mrs Smith, Mrs Smith would be committing treason and be put in jail for life if she damaged Post Office property. Better to have a cup of tea and a good cry in the Post Office kitchen which is what Mr Jackson had done yesterday when he came to post a registered letter.

'And you, my girl,' Miss Beach turned on me, 'you make yourself scarce, this is a grown up matter, not for nosey-parker little girls.'

My best dream, the one which was definitely going to happen when I was grown up, was that I would sit around reading or dreaming all day and all night and no one, not even Mum, would say a word. They wouldn't say a word because I was grown up and you didn't say those sort of things to people who were grown up.

Of course when I got to thirteen I realised that it was going to be a little while longer before I would be considered grown up. When I was eighteen maybe. But I had a few more things to dream about.

When I was grown up and had a daughter I would let her stay up as late as she wanted.

When I was grown up I would never growl or threaten to keep this daughter inside for a week because she'd talked too long at the gate.

When I was grown up I would let my daughter read anything she wanted and never take a book away because it was too old for her.

When I was grown up I wouldn't care if my daughter never learned about housework or cooking.

I never had a daughter, so these dreams were never put to the test. As for being grown up, fifty years later I'm still waiting. But the dreaming still goes on.

When I'm grown up I'll be very wise.

When I'm grown up I'll be very patient.

Huh!

Never mind, I can read about people who grow up. Evidently. Apparently. So they say. This must be what is meant by fiction.

Talk's cheap

Hello? Is that Renée? Oh, sorry, I've obviously caught you at the wrong time. Are you sure you're all right? You're panting very heavily. Oh, you've just rushed up from the compost heap where you've been emptying the vacuum cleaner? Really? You mean you actually do the vacuuming? And cooking, and cleaning, and ironing? Well. And gardening too? Goodness me.

Well, what I rang for was to ask you a favour. I'm Rose Grove and I met you at the readings you gave in Reefton five years ago. Rose Grove? Oh well, I suppose you meet so many people. Well, you'll be interested to know we moved from Reefton two years ago. My husband got offered a job in Porohiwi. And we're really enjoying being up north. Porohiwi's much bigger than Reefton, another 3000 people, so there's more scope for someone like me, someone involved in the arts. In fact my husband complains I'm hardly ever home, ha ha!

I belong to the Porohiwi Players, the Porohiwi Weekend Artists Group, the Potter's Circle, the Thursday Night Poets, and at the last Annual General Meeting I was elected secretary of the Porohiwi Literary Club. Which is why I'm ringing. I happened to mention to the members that you and I had already met so they thought it was better for me to ring as the ice had already been broken, if you see what I mean, even if I hadn't been the secretary.

I want to ask you a favour Renée. We were wondering if you would come and speak to our club Saturday night, in three weeks' time. The 14th? About your writing. And maybe read a little bit from *Willy Nilly*. A real scream, that book. Oh, you've written three more since then? How lovely. I must have missed them. Have to see if the library's got them. So many books come out these days it's hard to keep track, isn't it?

What kind of talk? Well, we thought we'd leave that up to you. Anything you like really. Feel absolutely free. How long? Oh not too long, we don't want to encroach on your good nature, do we? Say a couple of hours? For the first half.

Then we'll have supper and this will be an opportunity for some of our members to talk to you individually. They're interested in writing, you see. Well, they've actually all had some published in our Friday Arts Page, so they're not total novices. We thought it would be an opportunity for you to answer questions about publishers, maybe set up a few introductory meetings, that sort of thing. And if they have any problems, maybe you can put them on the right track. I know, for instance, that Esmeralda Grunthorpe is madly typing at this very moment, she's so determined to have her novel ready for you to read. It's called *Six Watch While the Lentils Burn*, after something Noël Coward said once, apparently. Esmeralda's very knowledgeable about writers.

Esmeralda's generously offered to put you up — she's a very kind woman, and we thought you might like to read her novel after you get home from your talk. Give her the benefit of your advice. Anything you feel needs rewriting, just put little notes in the margins? And you're not to worry that you'll offend Esmeralda, she's not like that, not a bit.

I'd better explain that her novel is perhaps more literary than your kind of writing and will probably appeal more to those who like to read the deeper kind of stuff, but, as I said to Esmeralda, even though you go in for the, well let's say the different kind of novel, and that's life and we all know that these people exist so why not face it, that's what I say, I've never been prejudiced, Renée, I want you to know that. Esmeralda's novel is about — and please don't take this the wrong way, Renée — ordinary men and women.

After supper we thought maybe you could wind up your talk and do a couple of readings. About an hour, all right?

How many do we expect? Oh it'll be a good crowd. At least ten. Porohiwians are very keen on their literature.

A fee? Well, as I say Esmeralda is more than willing for you to stay at her place. As you'll appreciate, we're a small club and we can't really afford to pay travel expenses but we thought a weekend in the country might appeal and you could kill two birds with the one stone, so to speak. Have a lovely homely weekend at Esmeralda's, I've told her you wouldn't want a fuss, and that suits Esmeralda fine, she's a very *relaxed* person, just takes life as it comes, you know. And there'd be plenty to eat at our do on the Saturday night so you could fill up then! Only joking! It's true Esmeralda's not one of your great cooks, but there's plenty of fruit around at this time of the year, isn't there, and it's a shame not to take advantage of it.

I'll be honest with you, Renée, we can't afford a fee. But we thought if we all contributed some jars of jam and a few eggs, that might appeal?

What do you think?

Oh I see. Oh I *see*. A prior engagement. Well, you writers lead such busy lives don't you. You're the tenth one we've rung and you've all had prior engagements. Well thank you Renée. Next time perhaps.

GARDENING WITH RENÉE III

If you want to hang on to even a tattered remnant of sanity you have to accept that lawns and couch grass have a symbiotic relationship. It's no good trying to break up this foreordained coupling. Remember what happened to the Montagues and Capulets? All those dead bodies when just a modicum of acceptance, or, as we say these days, bonding, would have had everyone living happily ever after. Either that, or rip the whole sodding thing out and replace it with tiles.

If a lover quotes, 'My love is like a red red rose', get rid of her/him. All the red roses I've known have been vicious, prickly, lethally wounding (I'm talking surgical stitches here) aggressors whose mission in life is to do grievous bodily harm to anyone who comes within a metre of them. Forget the deadlocks, the alarms, the pitbulls. Just plant red roses outside every window and collect the bodies on your way out. Even the beauteous Gertrude Jekyll — a not strictly red but wondrously rich pinky rose with a gorgeous scent (okay all you middle-class pedants, fragrance) — is, like her namesake, snappish, staunch, and very very sharp.

Remember, gardening will cost you money, time, ruin your joints, wreck your back, give you a much closer relationship with creepy crawlies than you ever wanted, and there'll be scars you'll carry to the grave. Forget alcohol, cannabis, hard drugs — you only have to see the crazed eyes of the people coming out of garden centres to realise that here is the greatest addiction of the lot. And there's no cure.

And always remember. Garden centres don't sell plants, they sell dreams.

Homophobia on the range

How do you do? Pleased to meet you. What was your name again? Oh yes, Renée. Yes, Bill gave me that book of yours to read. I must say I didn't enjoy it one little bit. I mean I can understand *men* being like that, but women! No, it's not right. Hope you don't mind me being frank. I'm like that. What you see is what you get. But you see what I mean, don't you? No? Oh. Well, really! There's no need to be rude!

See, that's what I mean — women like that, they're all so aggressive. I used to live about four houses down from two of them and there was a bit of a fuss among the neighbours, some of the older women were a bit, you know, concerned. And I must admit I agreed with them when they said they thought it would lower the tone and reduce the property values. So we took up a petition to present to their landlord. I mean surely they vet prospective tenants these days? And if they don't, it's time they started. Anyway we all did a lot of work, got most of the neighbours to sign. Of course there were a couple of, you know, libertarians I think they're called, and one so-called Christian who refused to sign, but the other eighteen did.

But all our hard work and tramping around was for nothing. It turned out they weren't renting! Yes, they'd actually bought the place. So there was nothing we could do. Oh no, they keep the place nice, gardens and lawns, but there's an atmosphere, you know? I've always been quick to pick up that sort of thing. I'm sensitive like that.

Look what they've done to the word gay. They've taken a lovely adjective and ruined it. You can't use the word now without that connotation. But at least it's better than the word lesbian. Makes me shudder just to hear it. And they've got such deep voices. I'm certain they must take lessons. No real woman has a voice like that.

And have you noticed how they're infiltrating everywhere? The police, the nursing profession, even the church! And now they want to get married. At first I thought they were only doing it to get attention. Then I heard, in strict confidence so please keep it to yourself, that some of them actually want a wedding ceremony! Oh you saw them on television and they told the nation that? That they actually want the same rights as married people? Next of kin, the ability to leave their property to their so-called partner, to take priority over children, that sort of thing? I mean, where will it end?

Let's just move away, shall we? I've just seen someone. Actually, oh God, it's so embarrassing. When I was younger I went to a party, and she was there. I'd had a bit to drink, that's the only way I can explain what happened next. Actually I couldn't remember a thing the next day but according to my friend, and various other people, I actually went up to her, put my arms around her and asked her to come to bed with me. According to my friend I had to be dragged away.

I think it was something in the punch. She probably put it there. They're like that. No woman is safe. Well of course I felt a bit down. No one likes to be publicly rejected. Even by one of them.

But I made up my mind. From that time onward, I've been very vocal about the harm they can do. I mean, if they can affect me like that, what would they do to someone more impressionable? It was all a long time ago, of course, and I've never told anyone till now, but every time I see that woman, the whole business comes back. I felt dreadful.

Oh no, I've never regretted marrying Steve. We've had our ups and downs — who doesn't — but on the whole I've been happy. Oh good, she's gone. Silly old me, I must have been holding my breath. And I think that was the bell. I'm looking forward to the play, aren't you? I like plays that are about real people. People like you and me.

Facts of life for lezzies

Remember that it's liable to give your colleagues in the office just a teeny bit of a jolt if you get all butch and crudely announce that you'll be late in tomorrow because you're taking your old lady out to dinner. Better say something sophisticated like, I'll be late in tomorrow because the woman I've been bonking for the last twenty years has booked us in to the Honeymoon Suite at the Park Royal and we'll be swinging from the chandeliers most of the night.

If you're a luscious lipstick lezzie and you're in the company of luscious non-lipstick lezzies just tell the darlings that you wear lipstick because it adds a certain *je ne sais quoi* to kissing. They'll be off to the Body Shop before you can say Rain Forest.

When feature writers, journalists, editors, start slagging us off again, it's because (a) their son, daughter, mother or father has just announced they're gay, (b) they made advances to one of us, but were rejected, (c) they're falling in love with one of us and they're scared, or (d) (yes!) all of the above.

When you set up house with your loved one, it is unlikely your family will give you a kitchen tea, a reception, a new toaster, a set of garden gnomes, or financial help with the deposit on the house.

If you don't know what a spanner, a hammer or a screwdriver looks like, you'd better learn.

Monogamy (contrary to what the great Robin Tyler said) is not a dark wood you polish.

When some religious fundamentalist insists that homosexuality is merely a lifestyle, a matter of choice, because there are members in his congregation who were once homosexual, and who are now happy heterosexuals and fathers of five, if you can be bothered, just say, of course there are, but what does that prove? There are many members of Queers United who went along with the heterosexual lifestyle because they were too scared not to, who are now relaxed and happy homos. So na-na-na-na-na.

You just don't understand

I don't know why you're moaning about charging market rentals for state housing. Rent rises can't be tied to income, that's going back to Mickey Savage's time and we can't have that. If tenants of state houses can't afford rent rises they can go to Income Support and ask for an accommodation supplement. Income Support never answer their phone? Well, I'm afraid that's nothing to do with me, you'll have to contact them yourself.

Yes yes yes, I know what you're saying. If the state (the landlord) puts up the rent and then the state (the landlord) pays an accommodation supplement so the tenant can afford the rent, why not just keep the rents low and cut out the middle man? Especially as they never answer their phone? Well, I'll tell you why not. That's a basically flawed simplistic argument which shows very clearly that you just don't understand.

It's pathetic to bleat on about the properties being paid for years ago. That's not the point, for heaven's sake. What is the point? The point is that state housing was an investment and investments have to keep giving a return — that's why they're called investments.

Look, only someone with their head in the sand would say that it wasn't a money investment. And don't give me that garbage about them being built on the principle of providing affordable houses for poor people. Times have changed. You don't understand.

Maintenance? Ugh. Well of course the maintenance costs are monitored. That's only sound business practice. It'd be crazy to let maintenance costs rise above a certain figure.

Some tenants have been in their homes for twenty years? *So?* Don't be stupid, of course they've paid their rent all that time, otherwise they'd have been kicked out. Yes, their understanding when they began renting a state house was probably different, but things have changed. You just don't understand.

There are some vacant properties, that's true. And we've sold off some housing stock, that's true too. But what's that got to do with it?

No, the state does not have a responsibility to house people. What about those who've been released into the community? There are boarding houses for people like that. They're happier with their own kind, anyway. Why didn't we leave them in the residential care, then? That's not my portfolio. You'll have to address your question to the appropriate minister.

It's a waste of time talking to you, you just don't understand.

Best friends?

What friend waits until you've served your visitors with the champagne cocktails and crostini topped with cream cheese, smoked salmon and a pinch of caviar (well all right, glasses of Cold Duck and Snax with slices of tomato) then pads into the centre of the floor, legs wide apart, and begins slurping all over her private parts? Granted she's an Aussie, but even so.

I ask you, what friend munches her dinner with such frenzied fervour that little bits fly out all over the place in a five-metre radius and there's always one piece she forgets, which lies on the kitchen floor until stood on by some unwary bare foot? What friend sniffs and drools all over that same kitchen floor because once, when she was eight weeks old, someone dropped an infinitesimal piece of grated cheese?

What *friend* noses her way into your crotch the minute you sit down? (And that's enough of that!) She has to wait until you're sitting down because she's too short to do it any other way.

What friend pushes her way into the bathroom to watch because what you do is so fascinating? And you're in the position of being unable to do any more than scream uselessly at her? What friend, I repeat, what *friend* then sniffs the air as though in seventh heaven? Visitors or the people she owns — it doesn't matter, she's not fussy.

Tell me, what friend comes on a walk to the river then spends most of her time peeing on other dogs' poo? You may very well have different expectations of friendship, of course, and not mind if your friend screams and whines when left to sit in the car (with the windows down) for five minutes while you dash madly into the supermarket, but it's something I take strong exception to.

Maybe your friends make a habit of digging in your garden and burying biscuits, plastic flowerpots, socks, earrings, even a nail buffer, but I have to say that mine don't, and if they did they would be crossed off my Christmas card list very quickly.

Okay, it's nice to be greeted at the door by a friend when you come home from work, or town, or even when you come in after deadheading the roses, but does she have to go on as though she hasn't seen you for a year and display this ecstasy by screaming, jumping up and licking you all over? (All right! Settle down please! This is a family programme!)

What friend sprawls beside you on the bed at the very moment when you can't bellow at her because you've already picked up the phone, and breathes so heavily and so hoarsely that the voice on the other end asks tentatively if this is a bad time to call?

What friend gallops up to anything recently or long dead and rolls in it?

What friend maintains a continuous whinging and grizzling if you put your walking shoes on and don't immediately set out on a ten-mile tramp?

I don't actually number among my friends those who lie on the carpet and fart silently and then, as the miasma sends everyone else choking outside, looks around enquiringly as if to say, what on earth's got into you now?

And if someone I knew jumped on the cat as it walked past, chewed its tail then screamed blue murder because the cat whipped round and belted them, I would start to entertain quite serious doubts about their suitability as a friend. Wouldn't you?

It is probably clear by now that I don't go along with the idea that dogs are necessarily our best friends. Lovable, irritating, entertaining, loyal, vacuum cleaners around food, yes — but best friends? Come on!

Ladies and gentlemen

Ladies and gentlemen, you may wonder why I am standing here with no clothes on. No, I regret to say, I have not been given the honour of being invited to speak on this happy occasion. I don't know the young couple, Clorinda and Luther, or their parents. I am not a relative or a friend, I can't claim acquaintance with anyone, and I certainly haven't contributed a present.

The reason I stand here before you is that I was taking a short cut through the grounds when I noticed you all sitting around looking a bit down in the mouth. Why anyone would want to look glum on such a happy occasion I simply can't imagine, but as there seemed to be a lull in the proceedings, I thought I would brighten things up.

You may be interested to know that last weekend I attended the Public Speaking Sans Terror Course, or PSST as us aficionados like to call it. It cost $1999.95, for the two days. Of course that included morning and afternoon teas so it was really a very good deal.

Looking at me now, you probably find it hard to believe that, before attending the course, I was an intensely shy person who jumped like a startled hare if anyone spoke to me. As for speaking in public, well, that brought me out in such a muck sweat at the thought of it that I would have to have a little lie down. Now, as you see, that reserve has completely gone. And I owe it all to PSST.

You may be interested to know that at the graduation we all promised we would practise PSST every week and do our best to encourage people to attend the course. This is my first PSST of the week. Now that I have your attention I want to open your minds to the value to your real self of attending a PSST course.

You may wonder what standing here in the nuddy has to do with PSST, but when I tell you that the very first thing you have to do when you're making a speech is grab your audience's attention, I'm sure you will understand and appreciate my motives. I may be quite wrong but I have a strong feeling that I have got your undivided attention. I am not, you can probably tell, a very experienced speaker, but I have been told that there is a kind of electricity in the air that tells you when, as a speaker, you have grabbed people's attention. I'm told that in those circumstances you can almost hear a pin drop. I'm happy to say that's the feeling I'm getting from you at the moment. And I want to thank you for that. It's very encouraging.

Actually, I have to confess I was really getting a bit desperate for an audience until I saw you all sitting here looking, as I said, a bit down, and decided to take the plunge. I'm glad I did, because you're all looking much more wide awake now.

My friends (you don't mind if I call you my friends, do you? I'll take those nervous giggles as a yes), I know, yes I do, I know what's going through your minds. You're thinking, who the hell does this rooster think he is, asking us to listen to a boring old speech? Am I right or am I right? Well, I will let you in on a secret. Speeches don't have to be boring. I am not boring you, am I? Thank you. I rest my case.

The trouble with modern society is that very few people are interested in listening to other people speak. We, as a society, have lost the great and noble art of listening. Especially listening to speeches. So I have decided to address the problem by spreading the news about PSST far and wide. I may be just one individual, but as we all know, a single individual can make a huge difference.

Let me tell you just a little about PSST. As I said, the letters stand for Public Speaking Sans Terror. That is, speaking in public without fear. You are possibly thinking you couldn't do what I've done. Let me tell you that, like everything else, the first step is the worst. A week ago I would have been just like you. I would have sat slumped in a chair staring straight ahead, looking as though I was listening intently, but inside I would have been a mass — it's not too strong to say a chaotic mass — of fears and anxieties. To put it bluntly, I would have been looking for an excuse to leave. Now I'm not saying you're in quite that state, but I want you to know I understand your concerns. I do. Because I have been there myself.

Just to set those fears at rest I want to invite you all, yes even Clorinda and Luther, to a pre-PSST Course function to be held this evening in this very building, room 13. Tutors and some graduates will be on hand to offer information and advice. To whet your appetite I must tell you that everyone who attends will be given a ticket. One of these tickets will have the lucky number which will entitle you to a free place in next weekend's course. That ticket will be drawn towards the close of the evening. Now if that doesn't make you keen, I don't know what will. Just an informal occasion.

Five to seven pm. Drinks and nibbles will be served and dress is casual.

In conclusion let me urge you all to attend. Hopefully I've said enough to give you just a glimmering of what lies in store for you if you decide to attend. I'll see you there!

NEW YEAR'S REVOLUTIONS II

Out queers will be given free coffee for the rest of their lives, out lesbians to get cream with it as well.

Elections will be abolished, along with parliamentary pensions. Names of all people over twenty-one will go into a lottery. The first thirty names to come out (no I don't mean it *that* way — but it's not a bad idea, is it?) will win three years as Members of Parliament. A second lot of ten names will head Treasury, New Zealand Post, Housing New Zealand, Social Welfare, Health, Transport, Education, Arts, Foreign Affairs. Then they'll be left to get on with it. A cost-saving system which should appeal.

Every home in the country will be given a spa pool, and immersion for thirty minutes every day from 6.00 to 6.30 pm will be compulsory.

I will learn to let sleeping dogs lie.

Every woman who has been a mother, solo or not, for more than three years, will be given an all-expenses-paid holiday to the location of her choice. Alone.

I will be invited to pick the next Pope, in which case I suspect it will be a woman and her name, should she be crazy enough to think the cozzie's worth it, will be Desiree or Magda.

Conifers will be banned.

All concrete footpaths will be replaced by lawns and will be mown weekly by city councillors. At least then we'll know they're earning their keep.

The dictionary entry for Lesbian will read: *Strong independent woman who loves other strong independent women.*

The sound of music

What do you mean, do I like music? Of course I like music. I can't remember a time when I didn't sing or dance to the radio. When I was at school I enjoyed singing in concerts. I even liked galloping around the playground to the bellowed directions of the teachers as they tried to teach us the set movements of The Lancers to the tinny sound of the gramophone.

What really broke their hearts and left them sobbing wrecks on the asphalt was when they attempted to teach us the movements, words and music of a folk dance called 'Captain Jinks'. Simultaneously.

'I'm Captain Jinks of the Horse Marines' — No no no, Api! You don't go back, you go forward! Renée! If you don't stop giggling you'll go back to the classroom and write 1000 lines. Everyone! Are you listening? When I say start, you step out with your RIGHT foot. What? Who else doesn't know their left from their right? Oh God. *'I feed my horse on pork and beans . . .'*

I even had a leading role in a play. I was the princess stolen away by a tinker when she was a baby. Naturally I had to sing about it. 'An orphan I without a name' was the first line of this aria, after which a chorus of standard fives would obligingly roar in with, *'Poor orphan child.'* At the end of the play I threw off the black academic gown generously loaned by my teacher, to stand revealed in my young Auntie Olive's pink taffeta evening dress, which was thought to be something like the daily attire a princess might wear. It was made to fit by securing the excess at the back with a safety pin. 'Don't turn your back on the audience,' warned the teacher. Was he crazy? Would I turn away when everyone's attention was on me?

When my young uncles and their friends went off to war they had farewell parties and I heard them singing 'Mexicali Rose' and 'It's a Sin to Tell a Lie'. The war brought Vera Lynn and 'We'll Meet Again' — which always reminds me of the American marine who threw a packet of cigarettes from the back of the truck he was sitting in onto the footpath in Napier where I happened to be standing, and waved energetically when I picked them up. I wasn't very old and he looked about the same age as my brother, who was younger than me. It hadn't struck me till then how young most of them were.

I was sent to the Methodist Sunday School where I belted out 'Rescue the Perishing' with the best of them and swayed blissfully to 'I Come to the Garden Alone'. I was a great swayer. Give me an opening note and I'd start listing. I loved the grandeur of 'Guide Me O Thou Great Jehovah', and willingly attended choir practices for Sunday school and church concerts. I listened politely enough to Bible stories. I had to — I knew Mum would kill me if I didn't. (I didn't get pregnant before I got married either, because I knew Mum would kill me if I did. I wonder if the Health Department has thought of this method of contraception?) I learned my quota of texts, received my share of gold stars; when I was older I even read the Bible myself — but it's the hymns and choruses that remain.

Believe me, music and singing have been irrevocably entwined for me — especially when 'Ten Guitars' is being played. I don't mind warbling along to 'Sad Movies Always Make Me Cry' or sobbing into my sherry while I plead, along with a young Kris Kristofferson, for someone to 'Help Me Make It Through the Night'. Even Leonard Cohen singing (?) 'Suzanne' can add a certain hysterical spark to my evening in the right circumstances. I know every word of Janis Joplin's 'O Lord Won't You Buy Me a Mercedes Benz', and hum along very happily when Peter, Paul & Mary sing about 'Puff The Magic Dragon'.

I can even go back a few years and join in with Bing Crosby when he sings 'White Christmas'. Just the first time, though. After that I turn him off. Anything Ella Fitzgerald sings, of course I listen to, in complete reverent silence, as is her due; and when she, Louis Armstrong and I get together — well, as you can imagine, it's magic.

I think the Finn brothers are great, but then their parents had parties where people sang, so they would be, wouldn't they? I have to grin when I hear The Cat's Been Spayed do 'Down the Hall on Saturday Night', I love Tom Waits and 'The Piano Has Been Drinking' and k d lang only has to sing one note of 'Hush Sweet Lover' and the cat and the dog know that it's time to dance.

I wouldn't call myself a classical music fan, because I don't really know much about it. I know when I hear a lot of violins and the odd French horn that it's probably a symphony orchestra. When I turn on the radio and someone is complaining in a high-pitched voice that their hand's a teeny bit cold, I have a feeling it's something operatic.

I read somewhere that baroque music is a good stimulus for the brain

— makes it zing along like stink apparently — so I bought a couple of tapes and played them, humming to the tune (yes, Virginia, baroque music *does* have a tune) and eating bananas, also supposed to be pretty good fodder for any tired old brain cells I've still managed to retain.

I stopped doing this because people gave me funny looks on buses. I think people on buses don't worry too much about the health of their brains. They're enjoying having a wee rest from all the hurly burly that we call living. They're not crazy about smart alecs who sit at the back of the bus listening to music. I think it makes them feel guilty about slothing out as they race from one high-powered appointment to the next. If the smart alec with the earphones starts humming and waving bananas, it only adds to their psychic discomfort.

But whether they'd admit it or not, their brains obviously do start working. A lot of them remember appointments they'd nearly forgotten, and get off at the next stop. I know, because they tell other people on the bus who also remember an appointment. And then there is just me and the bus driver left on the bus. Turn it up, she says, so I do. Hooray for baroque music! But only in the privacy of my own home.

The point I'm making is that I'm programmed to like all kinds of music. I'm not prejudiced against one sort or another. I'm not. Whether it's Elvis singing 'Love Me Tender' (yes, I know, yukko, but there's a memory there, okay?), dance music (rock and roll or foxtrot, I'm not fussy) or music that you sit and listen to, I'm happy. I'm quite prepared to clap to the beat if urged on by someone up front, and have been known to draw quite a complex vibrato out of the old tissue and comb if given the right encouragement.

Okay, you've won, I admit it! THERE IS ONE KIND OF MUSIC THAT REALLY GETS UP MY NOSE!

I'll give you a clue. It's two o'clock in the morning. All of a sudden there's a bunch of musicians in my bedroom playing very loudly. They are accompanied by John Rowles singing 'Cheryl Moana Maree' right into my left earhole. Or there's a rappie, and he's telling me, very loudly, about COP FUCKING CORRUPTION. Or someone is trying to repair their brain cells with a bit of old baroque and Handel's *Fireworks Suite* is exploding right through the house.

Yes, you've guessed it. Right on the button. I HATE LOUD MUSIC!

I know that consideration for others is not a post-modern concept, because postmodernists don't believe others exist anyway, so there. I know that there are people who determinedly live in post-feminist times. They also have a sneaky feeling the earth is really flat. But are they so bitter and twisted that they have to play 'I Am Woman' at 150 decibels so they can then discuss whether it's too retro for words, or whether it was really an ironic comment on the nature of Western society?

I know that anyone under fifteen has problems grasping the fact that when you live in a community, some consideration for others makes the world a happier place. But playing loud music is not confined to just one generation.

Okay, let me set you the scene. Me sitting in my garden this Sunday afternoon reading an old Margaret Drabble. (I love Margaret Drabble. I love her discursiveness. I hate everyone else's but I love hers. Hers is witty.) So there I am. The lawns are done, the garden relieved of its weeds, the roses watered.

Beside me on a table are a large gin and tonic and some homemade crostini with homemade pesto. Very couth. Seated at the other side of the table is my Significant Other. Yes, I'm at peace with the world. All is calmness and tranquillity. I smile at the roses, which are now aphid-free because earlier I went berserk with a garlic, chilli powder and grated soap spray. Life is good.

Into this idyllic scene a tenor's voice suddenly booms. 'I'll walk with Gard' blasts out over the air, and the ice in my gin and tonic cracks shrilly.

Mario Lanza?

Are you mad?

Probably, but it's still Mario Lanza.

Next thing I hear Howard Morrison doing his commercial for 'Grenada'.

Oh, I see. You were having your sixtieth wedding anniversary bash and thought in the circumstances the *neighbours* wouldn't mind. You're very upset a *neighbour* had been so *unneighbourly* as to complain. Tell me, have you ever complained? Oh you have. When the kids down the road played their stereo too loud. Oh I see. That was different. That was *them*.

Yeah, right.

Hello? Is that Noise Control?

Et tu, Brute

Dear Brutus,
I am desperate. I have loved a man for many many years. Three years ago he left his wife (or she left him, let's not quibble), and a year later they divorced. I wanted to marry then, but he said to be patient, the timing had to be right, otherwise he might lose his job. He said not to worry, one day we would be married. In the meantime, to tidy things up, I got rid of my husband and all looked set for a happy ending. Then his former wife was killed in a car accident. Now I'm afraid the timing will never be right. Will I ever live openly with the man I love?
Yours-from-a-sea-of-troubles, not drowning but waving (wearing a white glove hopefully!), Camilla.

Dear Camilla,
You win some, you lose some. That's life. Don't sit around moping — a trouble shared is a trouble halved. You think you've got troubles? Try striking up a correspondence with Edward Kennedy.
Good luck! Brutus.

Dear Brutus,
I am a clairvoyant. Recently, during a séance, an Italian Spirit Guide from the Other Side, called, I think, Julius (his accent made communication just a teeny bit difficult), asked me to write to you and say, 'Just wait till you pass over, you traitor, you arsehole, you pig's balls you! I'll be the one heaping coals of fire.'
Yours, Idesov March.

Dear Idesov March,
I only did what I was told. He understands how these things work. He did the same himself. All the above are quotes from the Book of Common Phrases for Politicians given free to every new member, which he knew OFF BY HEART.
Up yours, Brutus.

Dear Brutus,
Our club, a male preserve since Jesus played half-back for the Israelis, recently voted to continue to admit only male members. Since then my wife has declared our bedroom a female preserve and refused to allow me entry. I've explained until I'm blue in the face but, being a woman, she cannot seem to grasp the difference between public and private life. What can I do?
Yours, MCC Member.

Dear MCC Member,
Well mate, as they say in the cricketing world, LBW is not just an acronym for Leg Before Wicket. Looney Bloody Wanker or Lyophilic Blockheaded Weasel also spring to mind. Maybe you could ask Bill Clinton for advice.
Brutus.

Constance Spry and I

Flower arranging has not been one of my consuming interests. I know, however, the thrill of achievement and pride that comes when you place just the right flower in just the right place and there in front of you is a perfectly shaped and balanced composition. Yes, I have been there. Only once, it is true. But, as Somerset Maugham said, you don't need to eat a whole sheep to know the taste of mutton. One single chop will do.

I am referring to the days when I was a member of the Women's Division of Federated Farmers, Ponsonby Chapter. We weren't officially affiliated to the parent body. I'd be surprised if WDFF even knew about this particular offspring, but there's nothing world-shatteringly new about that, is there? It's a wise parent, etc etc. We settled on the name because some of our members were country girls and had fond memories of WDFF meetings, because we were sick of arguing about names (feminists spent a lot of time arguing about names in those days), and because our other option, the Ponsonby Gas Co, could be misconstrued.

The inaugural meeting of the WDFF Ponsonby Chapter was held in the Domain in Auckland so the SIS couldn't overhear us. In those days the SIS had an intense interest in people who worked on *Broadsheet* magazine. Two of our WDFF Ponsonby Chapter members were on the collective. Therefore we were all suspect. Or so we thought.

The WDFF Ponsonby Chapter was to be a social club. We were all agreed. Some harmless fun was what we wanted. We were agreed. Getting slagged off because you want to change the world can be a bit tiring at times. So as far as WDFF Ponsonby Chapter was concerned, Frivolity Rules, OK? But what would we actually provide for members?'

'Dances?'

'That's the whole point isn't it? So we can dance together?'

'Meetings.'

'Suppose so.'

'Speakers? '

'Only if they're not boring.'

'Competitions?'

'Competitions?'

'Yeah. Competitions. You always have competitions at WDFF meetings.'

'Really? I thought that was Women's Institute.'

'Them too.'

'What kind of competitions?'

'Well. You know. Three scones on a plate. A cream sponge. The best sausage rolls. And after the judging we eat them for supper.'

'Judging?'

'Of course. You've got to have first, second and third, plus a couple of highly commended.'

'Feminists don't judge, do they?'

'When it's three scones on a plate they do.'

A whole new world was opening up for the city girls. They got very excited. I'm talking radical feminists here, both lezzies and hets. They rolled around pounding the grass, hiccuping and gasping and pleading for mercy. But in the end they agreed.

'We'd better have a sand saucer competition.'

'Sand saucer?'

'Gotta have something for the idiots, sorry, I mean those who can't cook.'

'You shouldn't be so ready to criticise, Renée. They've probably had an unhappy childhood.'

'Yeah? It might interest you to know that my childhood was worse. We lived in a shoebox in the middle of the road. So there. And I can cook.'

'Yeah?'

'Yeah.'

Heavy feminist stuff, eh?

We elected a Madam President. You always have to have a Madam President, apparently. There was only one of us who had a satin evening dress, a fur stole *and* a string of fake pearls, so she was elected unopposed. For the first social event, Madam President's mother, it was agreed, would be roped in as the judge. This meant that Madam President would not be eligible to enter, but she was going to be busy looking for a tiara, so that was okay.

Now is the time to reveal a severe character flaw. I know this will come as a shock to those who thought I was perfect. Let this be one of Life's Great Lessons. There has only ever been one perfect person, apparently, and he lived at home with his mother until he was thirty-three, when he suddenly decided he was God. Like a lot of people in this state he received very little in the way of support, started hanging out down at the beach with a few so-called friends, and ended up in a very sad way.

My tragic flaw is that, like Macbeth, I am a very competitive person. There I've said it. I like to be up there with the best. Preferably in front of the best. And I'm inclined to sulk if I lose because I'm a very bad sport. So. No prize for guessing who was going to go all out to win every WDFF Ponsonby Chapter First Social Event Competition.

We hired a hall in Ponsonby. Invited friends and family from the country, friends and family from the city. Madam President located a three-piece dance band, piano, drums, saxophone. I interrogated them about their ability to play waltzes, foxtrots, Gay (well, of course) Gordons.

'You can't have country people here without a Monte Carlo and a Military Two-Step,' said a country voice.

'What the hell's a Military Two-Step? We've got a group coming from Women For Peace, remember.' City voice.

Heavy stuff.

Very political.

What about the competitions?

Three scones on a plate. Cream sponge. Four sausage rolls. The best sand saucer. A floral arrangement – theme; I am Woman. The best speci-person flower. (We laughed like kookaburras when we thought this up. Yeah all right. It was the early 80s, okay? We hadn't quite cottoned on that the only people who enjoy feminist jokes are feminists. Call us naïve, but we were astounded when our flippancies against ourselves were taken as serious political statements and used as evidence of excessive political correctness. But we learned. Oh, how we learned.)

I hired a tuxedo. Looked up the *Edmonds Cookery Book* for recipes for scones, sponges and sausage rolls. Bought sausage meat, pastry, eggs, cream, flour, cornflour, cheese (for the scones, stupid) and baking powder. Plus my list of secret ingredients. Got them all assembled on the bench. Rushed down to Pt Chevalier and got a cup of sand. Looked for a saucer. There were no saucers — everyone used mugs. Mugs don't come with a saucer. I finally bought a saucer (why didn't I use a plastic lid? Because a plastic lid is not a saucer) from a secondhand shop along Ponsonby Road. I damped the sand and poked some white daisies and purple pansies into a double woman's sign. Then I made the scones, the sponge, the sausage rolls. All perfect, as you would expect. There remained only the floral arrangement.

I repeated the theme over and over, hoping for inspiration: *I am Woman.*

I am Woman. How could I represent this, loaded as it was with historical, political and social connotations? Women had written essays, articles, books, made films, produced plays. They'd painted stunning canvases, sculpted, made music. All on this very topic.

I had three yellow marigolds from the neighbour's garden, one of which would have to be the speciperson flower; a few leaves of flax, ditto; and a rather prettily shaped glass jar that once held tomato relish, which I'd bought for $1 from the Lesbians for Peace stall. How could I hope to come within cooee of these achievements with such meagre resources? *I am Woman.* If I repeated it a few hundred times, maybe my subconscious would kick in and present a creative idea.

It was a great night. My scones came third, my sponge was highly commended and some greedy-gutses ate my sausage rolls before the judge could get at them. My speciperson flower came nowhere, but I didn't expect it to. When it was time for the floral arrangements to be judged, my subconscious finally came up with an idea.

No, I thought. No, that's silly.

Got any better ideas?

Haven't got any ideas at all.

You got nothing to lose then, have you?

I leapt up on stage. And stood. Something like the Statue of Liberty, only shorter. A marigold behind each ear, the flax leaves held high. '*I am Woman,*' I roared. Some people laughed, but I stood my ground. My very own floral arrangement.

The judge gave me a special prize — for ingenuity, she said. For cheek, everyone else said. But hey, a prize is a prize, I reckon.

Camping

It's not just that I'm a sugar baby who likes my comfy bed with four pillows each, a floor with carpets, a refrigerator and washing machine, a flush toilet and shower. It's not only that I like to cook, and that I've slipped into the habit, old hedonist that I am, of doing it on an electric or gas stove with oven. I know I'm working-class, but I like running water. And I'm sorry, but I can think of better things to do than being eaten alive by sandflies or bitten to death by mosquitoes. I like mushrooms, but I'm damned if I'm going to enter a paddock where two bulls are grazing just so I can experience the taste thrill of wild mushrooms cooked over an open fire.

You will have gathered that the joys of camping have passed me by.

People who love camping are always coming home with broken legs because they couldn't wait to get out under the full moon and dance over the sand dunes. They get broken arms because they slip, while running, on a wet wooden bridge they'd just told the kids not to run over. They suffer broken collar bones from getting tangled up with a tent pole; broken toes from dropping the gas bottle on their foot. No need to mention the burns from spitting fat, the gashes from the tomahawk which mistook their leg for a piece of willow, the infected sores from the bites they scratched. Or the virulent dose of hayfever from the Russell lupins growing wild along the verges, which takes a month and some very expensive visits to the doctor and pharmacist before it disappears.

When people go camping it always rains and the river rises and they have a sick child and they can't get to the doctor. Or there's a cyclone which picks up their tent and their car and, like Dorothy and Toto, they don't see these items again for months. And then they're informed that the items have been found in Gore, and they either have to get themselves down to Gore at their own expense, or pay a driver who takes a month to return their vehicle because he's seized the opportunity to do that tour of the South Island he's been dreaming about for years, and this seems a golden opportunity, with you paying for the petrol and accommodation. His wife needed a break, and as far as the kids are concerned, it's educational, isn't it?

People who go camping are always thinking about going camping. The snow can be thick on the ground, the trees bare, the rivers swollen to tsunami size, and they're planning a camping weekend in the Catlins.

'Great scenery and no fire ban at this time of the year.'

'Choice.'

'And, darling, it's the perfect chance to try out our superduper rainproof, tornado-deflective, double-quilted, lambswool-lined, double sleeping bag. What do you say?'

'Let's do it!'

People who enjoy the challenge of sleeping on rocks, who positively welcome visits from wetas and katipo spiders, who set their watch alarm so they won't miss a note of the dawn chorus — they're the ones who jump up and down with ecstasy when they spy an old kerosene lantern in a secondhand shop. No matter that their garage is filled with old kerosene lanterns — they simply must have this one. Maybe it will have that absolutely essential hinge or screw or fitting that will make all the other old kerosene lamps workable. And maybe I'm Ali Baba.

People who pack up the car at the drop of a hat — or at the suggestion that it's their turn to cut the hedge — just love the simple life. They slaver over packets of dehydrated mince. You can hear their shouts of joy from as far south as Stewart Island, when they discover a new kind of dried brains. They're the kind of people who actually make a study of tripe and can (and do) tell you all about the nutritious gains to be made by eating this muck for both breakfast and dinner. Just add water, bring to the boil, and away you go. No salt, of course — salt's bad for you. Don't worry about the grey colour; just shut your eyes and think of England. And now, yippee, they've found a supplier of dried tripe, so they won't have to go without their favourite food while they're on the road.

The thing I dislike most about campers is that they're so *cheerful*. Their tent gets slashed to ribbons by a passing deer; their kids turn from happy well-adjusted children into whining mad-eyed monsters; their spouses change from mature, loving individuals into nagging gaunt-eyed human beings with a bad back — and still they insist that the family loves camping. They're the ones who know all the campfire songs, and get all cold and withdrawn if others don't join in for just one more chorus of 'The Happy Wanderer'.

It always puzzled me why they regarded camping as such a treat. Now, after years of research, I've finally worked out why. After a fortnight away camping, the sagging piles (yes, all right!), the holes in the roof, the ill-fitting windows of the old homestead hardly impinge. Yes, after days spent doubled over like a staple to accommodate a backpack, three nights unable to breathe until the three people lying next to you turn over, home, whatever its shortcomings, feels like a palace. If you've been to hell and back, a few draughts or the odd loose floorboard or even a window or two that won't shut are neither here nor there. You're under cover. You haven't had to put it up yourself. And you don't have to get up and take the kids to the hole in the ground in the middle of the night.

Yes, okay, if you'll just stop pushing my arm up my back, I'll admit I'm a prejudiced old bat, and camping is really a wonderful people-centred activity where the whole family gets to grips with Nature and finds out things about themselves they would never have believed.

Okay. But . . . fantastic when you stop, eh?

The good old days

Long drops, dunnies, corrugated iron outhouses.

Squares of newspaper.

Filling the copper with buckets of water from a tap (if you were lucky enough to have a tap) usually situated about a mile away.

Flies swarming around the meat safe.

Rancid butter.

Warm thick milk.

Props falling down from a line of newly-washed sheets so the sheets drag on the muddy ground.

Beating carpets hung over a line outside.

No rubbish collection.

The Night Cart Man.

Digging a hole and burying the contents of the lavatory can when it's too full to wait for the Night Cart Man.

Queues for food.

Six o'clock closing.

Nah, give me the bad new days.

An hour with . . .

Ladies and gentlemen, it's my pleasure and privilege to be here today at the Porohiwi International Arts Festival and to introduce to you our guest speaker, who has travelled all the way from Wellington to be with us today.

Before I do, here are a few housekeeping notices I've been asked to pass on. Now, nothing personal, but the Fire Officer has requested that those people sitting on the floor in the front here please leave. Immediately. Yes, that does mean right now. I'm sorry, I don't know anything about refunds, you'll have to ask at reception. And to you too, Buster!

Coffee and tea will be served on the mezzanine floor after this session, and there will be a charge. I've been asked to make that clear. *There will be a charge*. Apparently there was an unfortunate scene in the last interval resulting in two arrests, and our Member of Parliament was taken to hospital with a fat lip. We don't want a repetition of that, do we? How much are the sausage rolls? You'll have to ask at reception. Other food? Yes, food other than sausage rolls will also be available for those who require sustenance, ha ha. Although looking around, I would venture to suggest that we could all do with less food, ha ha.

I'm sorry you feel like that. It was a joke. Excuse me, I *said* it was a joke. Well, I'm sorry. You eat all the sausage rolls you like, and if you have a heart attack at forty, don't blame me.

There are still tickets available for tonight's hour with the standup comic Stinko McPlug. No, I've never heard of him either — but then, I'm not interested in filth. What was that? He does religious impersonations. What do you mean religious impersonations? He impersonates Christ? He walks on a bath of water? Good Lord. And he does Mary? And how does he do that, may I ask? He puts on a wig and a blue apron. He does the odd fisherman as well? How odd. Interesting. Please see reception if you want tickets. How much? You'll have to ask at reception. Time? Ask at reception. No, I haven't got a tape in my pocket saying '*Ask at reception*'.

I'm sorry you feel like that. I'm merely reading out these few notes because I've been asked to, all right? If you think I accepted the invitation to introduce our guest speaker, who is waiting so patiently — thank you so much, it won't be long now — simply because I craved an opportunity to read out a list of stupid requests and notices, then you've got another think coming. I've got better things to do with my time.

The last notice concerns a red Honda, registration TQ9999, which is parked in the space reserved for the president. Would the owner of this red Honda please remove it before the towing company is called. And who are you, Madam? The President's wife. I see. Well perhaps you'd better take that up with your husband — this is really not the time or the place to discuss your private business. Whether everyone at this goddamn festival is talking about your husband's affair with the secretary of the Porohiwi Arts Festival Committee is neither here nor there, I'm afraid. You must remove your car if you don't want it towed away. Well, if it has to be over your dead body, then all I can say is, that is your choice.

It is now my very great pleasure to introduce to you our guest speaker for this session. Unfortunately I have to confess her name has gone right out of my head. All these notices, I suspect, ha ha. While I'm about it, I might as well confess also that I haven't read any of her books or seen any of her plays, so I can't speak from personal experience. And when I asked her just before we came on what she would like me to say, she just looked at me. Coming from Wellington perhaps accounts for this. However, I am sure she needs no introduction. And although I have not personally read any of her books, I'm told by those who should know — my darling son's teachers — that her work is of the highest quality. And that is what we all want, isn't it, quality? Unfortunately, it's the very thing this poor old country of ours lacks, these days. I ask you, where is the quality today? When was the last time you came home and said to your nearest and dearest, Well, I really had some quality time today.

Apparently our guest speaker explores the problems and issues in our society, and does it with a light hand and an observant eye. According to the notes handed to me, she went to school in this area. Well, really, I didn't know that. So she's an old girl of Porohiwi College. And I'm sure a credit to us all. It's not very often poor old Porohiwi can boast about its old girls, is it? But now we can. Ladies and gentlemen, it is now my very great pleasure to present to you . . .

Oh dear, she's gone.

A fairy story for baby dykes

Once upon a time there lived a baby dyke called Cindy Ella. All her life she'd been brave.

Cindy Ella lived in a three-bedroom townhouse with her two stepsisters Frankie and Johnny. Frankie was an area manager for a national corporation and Johnny was head of a girls' school. All their lives they'd been frightened.

They looked down on Cindy Ella because she worked as a waitress at a fast-food place. Cindy Ella liked working at the fast-food place because, although her arms, legs and smile were kept busy, her mind was free.

Cindy Ella worked all day at the fast-food restaurant, and when she got home she worked half the night doing the housework and washing because Frankie and Johnny had such hard, busy days, they came home haddit. One day she decided she'd had a gutsful of doing all the shitwork. And she'd had more than enough of her stepsisters. Two more bad-tempered dykes would have been hard to find. They got up grumpy, and went to bed worse. And in between times they moaned. The only thing that cheered them up was making Cindy's life a misery.

Why?

Cindy was young, but that wasn't why. She was good-looking, but that wasn't why. She was a better dancer than Frankie and Johnny, but that wasn't why. The reason Frankie and Johnny hated Cindy Ella was that she was Out. And that made Frankie and Johnny even more frightened.

'Stuck-up bitch,' said Frankie, when Cindy Ella marched in the Hero Parade with a placard around her neck which read 'Closet for Sale'.

'Thinks her shit doesn't stink,' said Johnny, when Cindy Ella went on television to talk about Coming Out.

'All right for her,' said Frankie. 'She doesn't know she's alive.'

'Bet she wouldn't have lasted two minutes in the 70s,' said Johnny.

There was no way of proving this, but Frankie and Johnny were sure they were right. Cindy Ella was spoilt, she'd had it far too easy, she'd always been her father's pet, and their mother had loved her too. It wasn't fair. Even when Cindy Ella came out, the father and stepmother hadn't faltered. They still smiled at Cindy Ella as though they loved her, and always told her to bring a friend when she came home for dinner.

'Bet they'd have locked the door on us,' said Frankie.

'No doubt about it,' said Johnny.

They glared at Cindy Ella as she vacuumed around the couches where they lay watching back episodes of *Ellen*. They'd stopped watching *Ellen* after she came out. It got stupid, they told each other. Lost touch with reality.

Now it's true that Frankie and Johnny had a point. The 70s, in spite of all the hooha about the second wave of feminism, were just as tight and confined as the 50s, when you lived in a small provincial town and you were frightened.

Frankie and Johnny had done the best they could. They'd worked hard, saved, and by the end of the 70s their combined savings allowed them to put down the deposit on this beaut house on a quarter-acre section in a rundown suburb of a big city. They'd done this with an eye to the future. Both of them had the feeling that one day the rundown suburb would be gentrified, although they didn't know that word then. In the meantime, no more worries about being kicked out by the landlord when the cops tipped him a wink. And being close to a big city meant that they could go out on Saturday nights without the local hoons breathing down their necks.

They'd saved money. Both Frankie and Johnny had faced facts early — mainly that if they didn't look after themselves, no one else would. When we're old . . . you know? In the meantime, keep your mouth shut, work hard, save, and we'll be safe.

They stuck together. Relationships were okay, but didn't last, they found. Sisters did.

Frankie and Johnny didn't go into the city a lot. You never knew when some demented dyke would pop out of a café and ask them for a donation for Lesbian Mothers, or make them sign a petition for Homosexual Law Reform, or beg them to come out.

They kept their high heels polished, made regular appointments for perms, put on another layer of lipstick. They made sure that everyone at work knew what they thought of feminists, especially the ones who marched for Gay rights; and they spoke approvingly when columnists slagged off lesbian preachers.

One day a tall handsome basketball player named Brickie arrived in town. Anyone who was anyone walked, crawled, hopped, skipped or jumped to watch her play. Oh the grace, the skill, the adroit handling of the ball! Those rippling muscles! The speed! The ease with which she danced, leapt, sprang from one end of the court to the other. She looked good, too. And her smile charmed everyone. Cindy Ella, Frankie and Johnny, and at least a thousand other dykes, all fell in love with Brickie and desired passionately to be her special friend.

The invitations went out to the Basketball Awards Ball. Many were the sighs, the moans, the screeches, that went up into the heavens, when the postie came and went and no precious invitation had plopped into the box. Frankie happened to be home with a migraine on the day their invitations were delivered. She ripped hers open and saw those wonderful words: *Brickie requests the company of Frankie*. At her very own table! The migraine left her instantly. Frankie clasped the invitation to her bosom. Then she looked at the other two invitations. Thought about it. Rang Johnny.

When Cindy Ella came home that night she looked through the mail on the table, but there was no invitation for her. Frankie and Johnny were all smiles as they showed her their own precious cards. They said, really kindly, 'Never mind Cindy Ella, yours will arrive tomorrow. Or the next day.'

'In the meantime, what are we going to wear?'

Over the next few days the house was in ferment as Frankie and Johnny brought home fabulous clothes, only to return them the next day because they didn't like them or because they were too similar. The Tweedledee and Tweedledum look was definitely not what they were looking for. They tried gowns, and smart matronly ensembles that usually pleased them because they didn't stand out, but nothing suited.

'Maybe it's time,' said Frankie.

'I will if you will,' said Johnny.

'Maybe we're too old,' said Frankie.

'Some people prefer older women,' said Johnny.

'You're right,' said Frankie.

So, taking a deep breath, they decided that, as well as the ball being the Basketball Awards Ball, it would be their Coming Out ball. Their clothes would tell the world who they were. What they were. They settled on very stylish sequinned waistcoats (one green, one red), black velvet trousers (one pleated in the front, one straight), white pintucked shirts, diamante spotted black bowties, purple (of course!) cummerbunds. And they spent ages practising their dance steps. Each secretly hoped to be the one Brickie would invite to dance the last waltz. And each felt a little frightened at the thought of coming out. Publicly. After all this time. They worried a bit about photographs, and TV cameras. But for Brickie, they'd do anything.

Cindy Ella polished and cleaned the house, washed and ironed, served supper and looked wistfully at the fabulous clothes which were hung on the landing because there wasn't room in Frankie and Johnny's wardrobes.

One night, after Frankie and Johnny had gone to bed to dream of dancing a slow foxtrot with Brickie, Cindy Ella sat at the kitchen table and cried. She didn't begrudge Frankie and Johnny their invitations, but oh how she wished she had been favoured too. She sighed and cried, told herself not to be silly, made a cup of tea, took a couple of Panadol, then cried some more.

Suddenly there was a knock at the door. Who could it be at this hour? Cindy Ella blew her nose and wiped her eyes.

'Who is it?'

'Your Fairy Godmother of course, you ningnong!'

'Who?'

'Don't muck around Cindy Ella, open the bloody door, it's freezing out here!'

Cindy Ella opened the door and there stood her very own Nanny, Maralda the Magnificent. She was tall, with flashing blue eyes and a stunning red wig. Her dress was the colours of a peacock's tail and around her neck was a bright green feather boa. Her fingers glittered with diamonds and sapphires. She waved her walking stick in the air.

'What's all the snivelling about?'

Cindy Ella told her.

Maralda's eyes grew hard and stony. She had been in hospital having a hip transplant, so her mind had been on other things. Naturally enough. But now, with her new hip, she was a new woman. A woman with a mission.

'Don't cry any more, Honey Chile,' said Nanny Maralda. 'You shall go to the ball.'

The night of the ball arrived. In Frankie and Johnny's bedrooms, there was chaos. Yells, telephone calls, hairdressers, showers ruining hairdos, deodorants, cummerbunds that wouldn't go round or wouldn't do up, bowties that wouldn't tie, last-minute spots on shirts, cries over laces breaking, some furtive farts, even more furtive use of Chanel No. 5. At last Frankie and Johnny were ready. They looked terrific. And Cindy Ella told them so.

Frankie looked at Johnny. Johnny looked at Frankie. Something that might have been shame appeared in both their eyes.

'Look Cindy Ella,' said Frankie.

'There's something you should know,' said Johnny.

There was a blast outside. Their limousine awaited. The chauffeur got out and opened the back doors and stood waiting, clasping and unclasping her white-gloved hands impatiently. She had other people to pick up. Neighbours, who had gathered to see them off, were in ecstasy. Limousines were not often seen in this part of suburbia.

Frankie and Johnny looked at Cindy Ella.

The chauffeur leaned into the limousine and gave the horn another blast.

'Catch you later,' said Frankie.

'Your turn will come,' said Johnny.

And looking just a bit regretful, the two left for the ball. They waved and bowed to their neighbours who smiled and waved back. 'We wondered about you two at first,' said one of the neighbours, 'but you're all right.'

'What did she mean?' Frankie asked Johnny.

Johnny shrugged.

The chauffeur seated them comfortably, opened the bottle of champagne cooling in the champagne bucket, and half-filled their flutes with pink champagne (what do you mean, sparkling wine? This is a fairy story, okay?), and off they went.

The minute their limousine disappeared, around the corner came Maralda the Magnificent. Behind her trotted a hairdresser, a makeup person, and a man called Fred who was carrying a beautiful white tuxedo. They swept past the amazed neighbours. 'Just you wait,' she said to them. 'You ain't seen nothing yet.' So said Maralda the Magnificent.

The hairdresser trimmed, brushed, blow-waved. The makeup person frowned over mascara, tried out this lippie and that lippie, scattered gleaming golden dust here and there, while Maralda the Magnificent walked up and down supervising. Fred indicated the white trousers, the white shirt, the white jacket. He laced up the white shoes, and when that was done, he handed Cindy Ella a white top-hat.

'Come here,' her Nanny Maralda commanded. She looked Cindy Ella up and down, from the top of her shining head to the tip of her whiter than white shoes. 'You'll do,' she said. 'But remember —'

'Yes, Nanny?'

'You must be home by midnight. Fred has to have these clothes back by 12.15 am. Get it?'

Cindy Ella nodded. It was only seven o'clock. Loads of time.

Maralda the Magnificent clapped her hands. She opened the door. There stood an open carriage drawn by two beautiful black horses. The carriage was painted white, with bright red upholstery.

To a chorus of ooh and aahs, Fred handed Cindy Ella up into the carriage, where a waiter called François stood. He bowed to the crowd, opened a bottle of Cloudy Bay Sauvignon Blanc — no diddly pink bubbles for François, thank you — and poured some of the precious liquid into a wonderful crystal goblet. Cindy Ella's eyes sparkled, she sipped and smiled happily. The neighbours smiled and cheered and waved.

'Remember,' cautioned Maralda the Magnificent, 'midnight, and not a minute later.'

'Thank you Nanny,' cried Cindy Ella.

'You're wasting time,' said Maralda. But she grinned her famous grin. 'Have one for me,' she said.

The ball was wonderful. Brickie took one look at Cindy Ella and danced every dance with her. They looked wonderful together. Brickie was wearing a black tuxedo and black patent leather shoes which shone as they danced. People just couldn't take their eyes off them.

Frankie and Johnny were miserable. This is what happened when you came out. They might have known it. All that money spent on these stupid clothes that they'd never wear again. They were deep in the dumps. People made such a fuss about coming out, but when you did, look what happened? There were flashes of cameras and Frankie and Johnny knew they'd look like halfwits with their eyes screwed up and their mouths open. But they'd still be recognisable. They'd thrown away their security, and all for nothing. Only the arrival of bowls of delicious smoked salmon, caviar on ice, thin toasted bread, some curls of lovely New Zealand butter, saved them from bursting into tears there and then. The crisp fruity Hawke's Bay Chardonnay helped a bit, too.

The prizes and awards were given out. There remained just the Super-Duper All-round Excellence Player of the Year Award. Everyone waited breathlessly. Cameras were pointed. Drums rolled, trumpets sounded. All eyes were on the stage. Cindy Ella glanced over at Frankie and Johnny and smiled. They didn't smile back. But Cindy Ella didn't care. This was the happiest night of her life; she wasn't about to allow a few hard looks from her stepsisters to spoil it. Then she saw Frankie's watch. One minute to midnight! Just as Brickie's name was called out to receive the Super-Duper, All-round Excellence Basketball Player of the Year Award, Cindy

Ella, with a broken-hearted cry, got up from the table and ran the length of the hall. One of the white shoes, laces loosened with all the dancing, came off. Cindy Ella stumbled, made a grab for the shoe, missed, and decided to leave it.

'About time,' growled Fred. As for François, he was doing very nicely, thank you, having polished off the rest of the Cloudy Bay plus a couple of bottles of the despised pink champagne left in the back of the limousine. Fred snarled, and slid François out onto the petunias (where he fell asleep instantly), climbed into the carriage, and got the horses moving. When they arrived home Cindy Ella ripped off the white tuxedo, apologised again about the missing shoe, and handed back the white top-hat. She knew that Frankie and Johnny would never tell Brickie where she lived because they were so pissed off with her. She went to bed and cried herself to sleep.

An hour later she was awoken by Frankie. 'Someone downstairs to see you,' she said gruffly.

'Yeah,' said Johnny.

Cindy Ella ran downstairs, and there in the sitting room, holding the white shoe, was Brickie. She smiled.

'Hello Cindy Ella,' she said.

They hugged and kissed and promised to love each other forever.

Frankie and Johnny came out of the kitchen where they had been eavesdropping, and they were hugged and kissed too.

'You must meet my sisters,' said Brickie to Frankie and Johnny.

Frankie looked at Johnny and Johnny looked at Frankie. Funny, but they didn't feel frightened any more. Is this what was meant by coming out? They smiled at Cindy Ella, and said they were sorry. Cindy Ella smiled back at them and said, 'That's all right.'

And they all loved happily ever after.

Just popped in to cheer you up

Are you awake? I thought you'd be awake. Walkie said you'd been out of theatre for a couple of hours. I rang Walkie and he said you'd come out about four. I was going to pop in tomorrow but he said I could come today, if it suited. So I left Doug doing the dishes, won't hurt him.

You're looking a bit tired. It was fairly straightforward, wasn't it? Nothing complicated.

Were you sick after the anaesthetic? I couldn't keep a thing down for days. But I've got a sensitive stomach.

I thought I'd come up today because, you know that sale we talked about, well, I saw a blue floral that I thought you might like. I thought you could do with a new dress. Got it on appro. They weren't too keen, seeing as it's a sale, but as I said to them, they can't expect you to leap out of your hospital bed and come downtown just because there's a sale on, now can they?

Anyway, it's a sort of powder blue with red and pink flowers. Cheerful-looking. I've always liked powder blue. And you like it too, don't you? It's buttoned down the front, and it's got pockets. Exactly what you need. Somewhere to put your hanky. Save you fishing around in your bra. It's a bit embarrassing when you start fumbling around in front there. People might wonder what you're going to pull out, eh? It's marked down from $120 to $80. Not a bad bargain, I thought. I mean, we all need one good dress, and that dark one of yours has seen better days, hasn't it? And I think this one might suit your complexion.

What do you think? I thought you could wear it to that afternoon tea dance we've been invited to. In a couple of weeks? Your hip should be better by then. You always seem to throw things off easily. Not like me.

Did you hear about old Mr Drabbe? Dropped dead. Just like that. He was in the kitchen, apparently, making the early morning tea, and after he'd been gone a while, his daughter went down to see what the holdup was, and he was sitting in a chair, staring. She got an ambulance but he died on the way to the hospital. Just shows, eh. Things happen quickly. A happy release, probably, although you can't say that, can you?

Now just say if you don't like the dress. There's no worry. I tell you what they did have that you would like — some of those pleated skirts. Marked down to $60. There was a lovely sage green one. I like sage green, and it goes with everything, doesn't it? Anyway if you're interested I could get it for you. You've got that nice green and brown patterned blouse with the fancy buttons I gave you, it'd look lovely with that. You remember you said you liked it, but you couldn't wear it because you had nothing to wear it with? Well, it'd look really nice with that skirt. Really good for the choir.

Doug's been a bit funny lately. Not talking. You know he has these spells of not talking. His father was the same apparently. He won a cup at bowls the other day. I don't mind him going to bowls, not like some. As far as I'm concerned he's perfectly free to come and go as he likes. I'm not one of these women who have to check up every five minutes.

Oh, I've just remembered. You know Mary? Mary Bolly? Her mother had a stroke. She was just lying in bed. Mary thought she was having her afternoon nap, and all the time she was having a slight stroke. She's not badly affected, shuffles along a bit, you know, and her speech is a bit hard to follow, but it just shows, doesn't it? You never know what's going to happen to you from one minute to the next, do you?

Well, I'd better go. I'll pop in tomorrow and see how you are. Always nice to have visitors, isn't it, and I've got nothing better to do. You feeling okay? Can't understand what you're saying, dear. Better go. Now you concentrate on getting yourself well. Bye.

To my two lost kilos wherever you are

Some grieve a lot
Some are bereft
But I hung out balloons
The day you left
You took your leave
Without goodbye
If I ever see you again
I'll scream and roar and yell and bawl and bang my heels up and down and have a bloody good cry.

I wrote the above for the *Lard Losers Letter* some years ago. It was a joke. Little did I know, heedless old me, that it would come back to haunt me.

In some circumstances (eating and drinking at expensive restaurants every night) I can agree that gaining weight is fun and almost to be expected. But what if I'm just going about my daily business, eating nothing but salads, walking the dog five kilometres daily, having cut even the gin out of the gin and tonic — and there, in front of my eyes, the scales are telling me this horror story?

It's true my trackpants have started to feel a bit tight and that's why I hopped on the scales. To find — oh my God, tell me it's not true — that, somehow or other, I've acquired an extra not one but two kilos.

Naturally I have the scales tested and they still say the same. I make excuses to go into strangers' bathrooms (a kidney infection, sorry!). I slither furtively onto their scales. Their scales (which obviously need attention) say the same. I know better than to try my friends' scales so, in desperation, I try the doctor's. The figures are there too — and not only are they staring me in the face, they're staring the doctor in the face as well. She even writes it down in her notes. I suppose this is the reason you're not allowed to see whatever it is that doctors write about you. The record of your weight gain and loss would be more than the strongest among us can take. No, this time I have to accept that, somehow, I've gained two extra kilos.

Where have they come from? I definitely have not been eating more than usual. I have not been slumping on the couch munching potato crisps, or leaning on the bench eating lemon cake and whipped cream. That woman walking along the riverbank munching on a stick of celery — that's me. Well, it was.

I know exactly what's happened.

Let me think. Who do I know who's been losing weight? Got it. That neighbour on the right has definitely slimmed down. I accidentally on purpose run into her at the bus-stop. Yes, she smiles happily, she's actually lost two kilos. On purpose.

I glare at her. I knew it. Two bloody kilos wandering around looking for a home, and bingo, I'm it.

I ponder bitterly whether it ever occurs to selfish beasts like my neighbour to wonder where the hell their lost kilos go. I mean, it's pretty damn selfish of people to lose all these ounces, pounds and kilos without even a moment's thought as to what's happened to them, don't you think? There they are, these careless yobbos, waltzing around yelling, I've lost two kilos, I've lost two kilos, and never even thinking where they might have gone.

Imagine it: all that excess weight lumbering around the world looking for somewhere to squat. It doesn't feel too good. Rejected by all and sundry. A deprived old time of it. Low self-esteem. Who will take it in? At last. *There you go. She looks kind. She won't mind an extra pound or two to feed.*

Well, I might look kind, but I'm not. I'm a cruel hateful mean person. I have no compassion, no sensitivity, no desire to make the world a better place for two unwanted kilos. I'm sorry. But that's just the way I am.

Most people advertise when they lose something: *Lost: A sapphire ring. Sentimental value. Owner bereft. Please ring.* You've seen the ads in supermarkets, on vets' walls. *Lost: Our dearly loved Jack Russell terrier. Answers to Bozo. If you see our darling, please call.* And there's a photograph of Bozo grinning.

Lost: On purpose. Two kilos of body fat. I'm sorry, I know we were close for a while, but these things happen. I enjoyed your company, but I've decided (I know this sounds harsh but) I don't want you any longer.

If you, the reader, see two kilos of fat looming about, please direct them to the nearest café. To put it bluntly, if I ever see them again it'll be too soon.

Even that would show some feeling, would be better than this fine improvident unheeding let-it-all-hang-out kind of attitude. *Hooray, I've lost two kilos.* Where have they gone? Who cares?

This attitude is what's wrong with the world today. This is what wears little holes in the rich fabric of our lives. Oh dear, I've lost something. Never mind I never really liked them anyway. And I can get some more if I need them. I wish them well, of course I do. But I don't want them back and frankly I don't care whether they find a home or not. If they have to trudge the world looking for someone to love them, so be it.

See what I mean? No care and no responsibility I think it's called. Meantime I'm walking around with two extra kilos that I don't want. And I've got this dilemma. I'm going to have to lose them. But how can I square it with my conscience? I'm not the sort of person who can just send parts of my body off into the ether without a moment's worry. Of course I worry. What will become of it? Where will it lay its head tonight? What kind of future lies ahead for it?

But hey — when the chips are down, it's every woman for herself, right?

So bugger off Kilo
And don't be a whiner
If you're looking for a home
Try Joe's Corner Diner.

HOUSEWORK WITH RENÉE I

I'm not surprised men have never liked housework. Who does? Who wants to do the same thing over and over and over again, knowing as you do it that it'll all have to be done again the following week? Or day?

I'll tell you who. Someone who has an aversion to dirty baths and basins, smelly toilet bowls, filthy floors, that's who. I'm funny like that. But it doesn't mean I like it.

I'm five foot four. I know that's short. I know it's short because I heard someone on CrimeWatch say so. They described a nasty crim, showed his face (he did look nasty, thanks), then informed us he was five foot four. And short, they added. As opposed to five foot four and tall, I suppose. Anyway, I concede that I'm five foot four and short, okay? But what I want to know is, why do people who plan kitchens always always always place one row of cupboards up so high that only a seven-foot-four giant could clean them with any degree of comfort? Because they're seven-foot-four giants and it seems normal to them, perhaps? The same reason bathroom mirrors are so high I expect.

I'm trying not to get bitter and twisted. I'm trying very hard, but I'm failing.

There's a new bath/toilet/floor/window cleaner out every hour, but they've never invented one that isn't improved with elbow grease. Funny that.

Why does everyone wait until the floor's wet before they walk through the kitchen?

Changing the clocks

October: second weekend. I think. You put the clocks forward. Now if this is not right, there's no need to write to me, get it? I don't care.

March: second weekend. I think. You put the clocks back. If this is not the right way round, don't bother to write to me. If you haven't already got the message, I don't *care*.

My heart sinks every time someone on National Radio reminds me, oh so cheerfully, that clock-changing time is coming up. For days I think of nothing else. Did they say forward or back? And if I set the clock back to nine o'clock when it's already been there, *what will it do to the clock's psyche*? If I forget and turn up either late or early for appointments, what will it do to *mine*? Naturally, being selfish to the core, my needs come first.

I hate changing clocks. I suppose my watch isn't so bad. It's got one of those little things on the side that you pull out to move the hands. I pull it out and get ready to alter it. I turn on National Radio and wait for them to tell the time so I can check my watch is correct. No sense turning it back (or forward) to the wrong time, is there? Of course, no one on the radio ever says the time when you're waiting for it. And they never ever say the time on the night you're supposed to be changing the clocks. Never. I tune another radio in to another station. They obviously have the same system: tell the time every two seconds, every day and night of the year, with the exception of the night you change the clocks. Then, don't mention it. Ever. It's a rule they teach them in Announcing Preschool. Well to hell with them.

Dear Announcer,
This is just to tell you that I won't be tuning in to your station any more, because, owing to your intransigence on the second weekend in March (you know to what I refer), I set my watch wrong and now I've been late for three important appointments. When your ratings decline you will know why.
Yours sincerely, Disgusted.

The clock on the microwave can never make up its mind whether it has to have the figures altered, or whether it wants you turn it off at the wall, then fiddle with its main buttons. Well, of course you have to turn it back on at the wall before the lights come on. I knew that.

You know the reason the people in charge of clock-changing leave it for six months before you have to change the clocks? It's all worked out scientifically. Six months is *just long enough* for you to forget how to change the clock on the video. This is probably very kind and sweet of the people in charge of this daylight saving business, because they know that a six-monthly argument about how to change the clock on the video is about the most a good supportive I-hear-what-you're-saying relationship can BLOODY FRIGGING HANDLE!

Have you noticed that when you change clocks you always seem to end up with one in the bedroom two minutes slow or two minutes fast? By the time you get to the bedroom you've been counting seconds for what seems like hours, and you tend to leap ahead or back; and before you know it, you've jumped backwards from 50. Forty-nine, 48, 47, 46 . . . Hey, haven't I just said that? Okay, now, I went four backwards, so that means I should be up to 54 — but I've also taken a second or two to think about it, so let's make it 56. Or perhaps we'll round the whole thing off and call it 60? So that's one minute. Now, what is ten o'clock in figures? I always get this one wrong. It would be so much easier if 10 became 20 instead of 22. But oh no, some dork — or dorkess, let's not be sexist here — decided that that would be too easy. So 8 becomes 20. So 10 is, what did I say 10 was? 22. Oh yes. Right, I've got it turned back to 9 (or forward to 11). How long do you think that's taken? Two minutes? Ok. We'll make it three, just to be on the safe side.

And that's how it goes. I'm thinking of writing a submission to the Daylight Saving Officers to plead with them to make it once a year. I don't think I can stand the present system much longer. Six months is far too short a time to recover. I need another six months for the trauma to subside, and for me to regain some optimism. I mean, hey, after a year, a little thing like changing the clocks will mean nothing. Like childbirth. The blood, sweat and tears, not to mention the curses and the agony (*Can you feel a little buzz down there? It's called pain, you fool!*) will have faded. Of course I can do it. I'll just use a few visualisations and a few thousand affirmations and away I'll go.

Yeah. And the Queen Mother doesn't have a walk-in wardrobe filled with feathered hats.

Why I like Auckland
(Well hush my mouth!)

Author's note: This is a memoir, so all characters and events are entirely imaginary. But it is true that this is an edited version of a talk I gave in Auckland in July 1997, at an evening called Diverse Divas.

Auckland, ah, Auckland, let me count the ways.

Auckland was where I finished my BA degree, came out as a lesbian, and began living with the woman I still live with. So sucks to all you people who didn't send us a pressie. Our love affair began with the two of us talking. She's Irish and I'm not, so we're still talking.

At the time I could see one important difference between me and other lesbians. No no no, *apart* from them all being young and thin. Other lesbians had big dogs — German shepherds, rottweilers, labradors, a doberman called Radcliffe — and I liked pekingese. But I'm making progress, sisters. I've recently got an Australian terrier so by the time I'm ninety I'll be about ready for a pitbull called Gertrude.

It was in Auckland that I noticed how many people had mugs with the word COFFEE painted on them. I was from Wairoa where we thought that, if you didn't know what a mug was for, you shouldn't be allowed near one filled with hot liquid.

Those were heady days of political action. Someone managed to sneak into the depot where the buses were parked overnight and scrawl Lesbian Nation on the sides of some of them. In the morning, no one noticed. This is not surprising, is it? Most of us take a few hours to open our eyes to the day. So the buses went out on the road, allowing lots of photo opportunities. You should have seen the faces on Queen Street. No prizes for guessing who was smiling.

Some actions were not so successful. I remember, one Sunday night, walking up Victoria Street, dressed in a pink picture hat with roses on it, a pink crêpe mother-of-the-bridegroom outfit, pink gloves, and carrying a pink purse with a brick in it. The brick was to be glued to the window of a particular shop which was displaying what I considered to be offensive pictures of women. Don't ask me why I was going to glue the brick to the window instead of chucking it through with a note attached. I had my reasons. Something to do with anti-violence, I expect. My friend Pat, in a rather loud red floral dress, was carrying the glue; and Jane, in a more subdued black ensemble, was there to keep a lookout.

A red Ford Falcon, left-hand drive, cruised past, circled and came back.

'What you got there? A gold brick?'

'Ignore him,' said Pat.

We walked on.

'You *are* Desiree?'

'No!'

'You look like her. Are you her sister Carmelita then?'

I shook my head and gripped the pink purse tightly. If he asked me whether I was Desiree or Carmelita's mother, I was ready.

'Aaah, what about a bit of the other?'

'What?'

'Well, I can tell, you know, you're dressed up for a good time, and I'm always a starter, if you get my drift?'

'Piss off, you stupid fuckwit!' I was past caring whether I drew anyone's attention or not.

'I said, ignore him,' said Pat.

'Shut up,' I said.

'Okay, be like that!'

We reached the shop.

I got out the brick.

Pat got the glue out and stood poised to pour.

Pat poured the glue onto the window.

I attempted to glue the brick to the window.

It wouldn't stick.

For about ten minutes we both held the bloody brick firmly against the bloody window.

It still wouldn't stick.

If you've ever thought about glueing a brick to a window, take my advice; it's not worth the effort. My hot sweats were having hot sweats.

I took the pink gloves off. Well I had to wipe my forehead with *something*.

'Don't take the gloves off,' hissed Jane.

'Why?'

'Your fingers will stick to the brick, stupid!'

We tried again.

For another ten minutes.

'For Christ's sake,' Jane moaned, 'hurry up!'

'You bloody try then,' I snarled.

'All I'm saying is hurry up!'

In the end we retreated, leaving the brick stuck to the footpath. Jammed up hard against the bottom of the tiles, of course. We didn't want anyone to trip over it and hurt themselves.

It was in Auckland that I began to write plays. It was in Auckland I decided to give teaching away, work part-time at *Broadsheet* and write the rest of the time. The other day I read in the morning paper that lesbians have a lot of disposable income but the only income I've got to dispose of, after paying my share of the mortgage, buying a few crusts of focaccia and maybe the odd bottle of wine on special — is five dollars, which is immediately invested in lotto. Well, they support the arts, so it's money well spent.

Maybe I should rethink that investment and give the five dollars to some of these chief executives who seem to need more and more money to help them keep up with the Joneses overseas. I notice that people on a good salary, paid into their bank account at regular intervals, often moan about the lack of money. They're the ones who can't send you a cheque for work done until they have a cheque run, which is usually about once every six months and then only when the moon is full. The first time I heard someone say, We'll send you the payment for this 10,000-word article as soon as we have our next cheque run, I thought they were talking about a marathon for East European runners. I spent days with my ear to National Radio so I'd know when they started off and my money would arrive. But I'm wiser now. I know what a cheque run really is. It's when they finally send me a cheque and I run like hell to the bank and deposit it before the manager starts frowning sternly at me. Yet again.

It was in Auckland I first heard talk about postmodernism. I didn't take too much notice. Besides I was pretty sure there's a law against posting modernism through the mail. I think it's just supposed to be letters.

Being a lesbian can be full of contradictions — and not just in Auckland. You probably heard the Nancy Mitford story about the Greek bishop who went to Buckingham Palace and the then Queen, now the Queen Mother, said, 'How do you do, very nice to meet you, I understand you're a lesbian.'

There's another good story about the Queen Mother when she was

Queen. She asked a Polish airman who'd come to the Palace to receive a decoration for valour from King George, 'Now tell me, what did you do exactly?'

'Well, Your Majesty, I shot down one Fokker and there were two more on my trail but I managed to shoot them down as well.'

'Jolly good,' said QM, 'and were they all Messerschmitts?'

But to get back to another lesbian joke. In 1934 when Lillian Hellman's first play *The Children's Hour* was presented on Broadway, it was a huge success. This in spite of the fact that its two main characters, teachers at an all-girls' school, were accused of being lesbians. The first time the L-word was heard on the American stage. Samuel Goldwyn from Metro-Goldwyn-Mayer couldn't wait to get Hellman onto the payroll of the studio as a screenwriter.

The first film adaptation she wrote was from a book chosen by Samuel Goldwyn and turned out to be a fairly ho-hum movie but people loved it and it made lots of money. To show his pleasure and delight Goldwyn gave Hellman total freedom to select whatever project she wanted for her next adaptation. Naturally she chose her own play.

One of Goldwyn's friends got into a terrible state, rushed up to Goldwyn and said, 'Sammie, Sammie, you've made a terrible mistake. That play has lesbians in it!'

'That's okay,' said Sam, 'we'll make them Americans.'

But back to dear old Auckland.

A friend of mine went along to a natural healer because she kept getting headaches. All she wanted was some safe sort of pill or liquid to deal with the problem. By the time she'd answered 1042 questions about her relationship with her lover, her mother, her father, her sister, her brother, her dog, her employer, then on to her feelings about Life and her response to the film *The English Patient*, my friend was so stressed she had to go to the doctor and she's been on large doses of Prozac ever since.

There was a lot of talk in Auckland about Bonding Weekends.

Bonking?

No! BONDING. Bon*dd*ing.

The idea was that if you hated and despised a particular person and she hated and despised you it was because, in the stresses and strains of the city, you two hadn't had a chance to *bond*. It was thought that, if you and the other person went away for the weekend to some place in the country with no inside lavatory, no electricity and no running water, the experience would see the two of you bonded forever. A friend of mine went along to one with a work colleague she detested and who felt the same way about her. When she got back I rang her up. How did it go?

'Chucked the bitch over the cliff,' she said.

It was in Auckland I had my first sip of wine. I didn't like it. At that stage, when I wanted an alcoholic drink, I had sherry and tonic. I bought the sherry in flagons from a little shop on K Road. A bottle of wine with your meal was a whole new concept. Where I came from you ate your dinner, or tea as we called it, and then you had a cup of tea or, if you were really daring, you made coffee with a teaspoon of dark brown liquid from a bottle labelled coffee and chicory, over which you poured boiling water. Plenty of sugar and milk and away you went. Delicious.

The Auckland literary scene was interesting if you were into blood sports. PEN meetings were famous for the pushing and shoving, the bitchiness, drunkenness, the backbiting, the fights — and that was just while the members were waiting for the one with the key to arrive and open the door. I'm told that's changed now. It all happens inside.

One thing I found disappointing about Auckland was the parties. No one sang. They had Holly Near and Joan Armitrading on the stereo instead. People sat on floors in the dark and talked earnestly to each other. They ate little bits of cheese on a water cracker with no butter, and there wasn't a saveloy or a bottle of tomato sauce in sight. They didn't even know the words to 'Ten Guitars'. I found out later what this disappointment meant. It was called culture shock.

It was in Auckland that I gave up smoking. Guilt finally spurred me on to do this. We both did it together. Cold turkey. The craving was worst at night, so I used to have a sip of wine every time I felt the urge to go over the road to the dairy and buy a packet of Cameo. I remember one night at a performance of *Camille* when I'd sipped so much wine by half-time, I was seeing Camille in triplicate. As you know, she spends a lot of time singing before she actually coughs her last.

'Why the hell doesn't someone tell her to go cold turkey?'

'Sssh!'

Auckland, ah Auckland. Those were the days. Well, some of them.

The day Mrs Ernie nearly went blind

One Sunday when I was out watering the marigolds I saw Mrs Ernie approaching. Reet always has marigolds and Salvia Bonfire along the front. She likes a bit of colour, does Reet. And I don't mind. Mrs Ernie loves the marigolds, reckons it makes summer for her. Anyway, as I say, I was out watering them when along comes Mrs Ernie. She was kind of not walking all that well and she had her arms out in front of her. Strange, I thought. But then I thought, well, she's a Mickey Doo Tommy boy. I'm a Methodist myself.

'Hello Mrs Ernie,' I said.

'Who is that?' she asked.

Well. I was a bit taken aback. 'Course I was. I mean, ask yourself. We've lived next door to Ernie and his missus for years. She knows who I am. 'Course she does. What was she playing at?

'Is that Tom?' asked Mrs Ernie.

'You know it is, Mrs Ernie.'

'Good,' she says. 'I thought it was your voice, but I wasn't sure.'

By now I'd tumbled to it. There was something wrong with Mrs Ernie's eyes.

'What's the matter?' I asked, and then wished I hadn't. I mean we all know how you go blind, don't we? Like, if you haven't been born that way or in an accident. I couldn't quite see Mrs Ernie going in for that sort of thing but then again, as I said, she's a Mickey Doo.

'I don't feel so good,' said Mrs Ernie.

Don't tell me, I thought, just don't tell me. I know that anything goes, these days, but Ernie and his missus and me and Reet have never been on those sort of terms. It was just a thought. And it was probably some woman's problem. And as far as I'm concerned women's problems should remain where they belong. With women.

'Reet's inside,' I said hastily, just to give her a hint in case it was something private.

'I've just been to see Father Gerald,' she says.

Shit, I thought. She's been to the priest to confess. I started to panic a bit. I mean what I thought was just an idle thought. Nothing serious. It couldn't be true, surely. Not Mrs Ernie. I mean she's my partner at 500.

'. . . and he said he's sure God won't regard it too seriously.'

Oh yes, I thought, that figures. Their God obviously doesn't have the same standards as our one.

'Reet!' I called loudly, hoping Reet didn't have the kitchen whizz on. You can't hear a thing when it's on.

'What?' Called Reet from inside. I mean Reet's had first aid training and I haven't. If Mrs Ernie, who I must say didn't look too good, was going to make a habit of carking it on our lawn, I wanted Reet there.

'Reet!' I called her again. The trouble with women is they never get the message unless it's spelt out. I mean a man would know I wanted someone there quick smart.

'What's the trouble,' called Reet.

'It's Mrs Ernie,' I said.

'Oh yeah.'

'Tell Reet, Mrs Ernie,' I said, moving away a little. 'She'll be out in a minute.' Under my breath I was saying come on Reet, come *on*.

'What's up?'

Thank goodness Reet had finally managed to get out here.

I gestured with my head. 'Mrs Ernie,' I mumbled.

'What about Mrs Ernie,' says Reet.

Women. I mean I could write a book about them. I frowned and nodded in Mrs Ernie's direction.

'I can't see properly, Reet,' says Mrs Ernie.

'Oh yeah,' says Reet. 'How long have you been like that?'

'Since last night,' says Mrs Ernie.

I moved away a little, but to tell you the truth I was all ears. You see Ernie was away last night. I know that because he'd cancelled the game of 500 we were going to have. Mother's crook or something. So that was it. Ernie away. I see. On a Saturday night, I thought to myself. I see.

'What happened last night,' asked Reet. You got to give it to Reet. At least she asks straight out.

Mrs Ernie shook her head. 'It was terrible,' she said. 'I don't know what came over me.'

I moved away. Listening's all right, but there are things you don't want to hear, not if you're intending to go on playing 500 with your neighbours. I took the hose around the side and concentrated on the bushes there.

'Tom! What're you doing?'

'Watering these bushes.'

'They don't need it. Just the front ones.'

'I thought yesterday how nice they looked,' said Mrs Ernie. 'And that's when I thought, Oh God,' she said, 'little do we know what's ahead of us.'

I looked at Reet. I looked at Reet imploringly.

'What's the matter with you?' Reet glared at me.

'Maybe,' I gestured with my head and shrugged my shoulders, 'maybe Mrs Ernie wants to be private.'

'Private?' Reet frowned at me. 'For heaven's sake Tom. You're not thinking —'

''Course not,' I said hastily. 'I just thought, well I just thought. No harm done, Mrs Ernie, eh?'

'No, no,' said Mrs Ernie. 'It's me that done the harm. I've made a fool of myself and if the world knows, that's my punishment.'

Reet said, 'Mrs Ernie tried to dye her hair with marigold liquid. She, um, borrowed some of these marigolds, boiled them up with water, and when she put it on her hair some of the stuff got into her eyes. She thought she'd give Ernie a surprise when he came home tonight.'

'He'll get a surprise all right,' said Mrs Ernie. 'I'm nothing but a wicked Jezebel, wanting to enslave my husband with golden tresses.'

'Now Mrs Ernie,' said Reet, 'I know you're in shock, but we'll have less of the drama, shall we? And you can stop standing there with your mouth open, Tom, and make yourself useful putting the kettle on. What you need, Mrs Ernie, is a cup of my strong tea.'

Later Reet said to me, 'I know what you thought, Tom. You should be ashamed of yourself. As if she would.'

'Dunno what you're talking about,' I said.

'Didn't think you would,' she said.

Pet accessories

Yes, I'm an addict. There, I admit it. It's not because of a deprived childhood or an unhappy life. I blame it all on the vet.

When you have animals you tend to spend an inordinate amount of time (and money) at the vet's. You get an eight-week-old puppy, it has to have injections. Well, of course it does. Are you a responsible dog-owner or what? Then it has to go to puppy preschool. Well, do you want it to be socialised or not? All right then. Socialising means it and twenty other pups tear around like out-of-control dodgems for sixty minutes while the vet lectures the owners on hygiene, training, feeding, and things to turn a blind eye to. For instance you turn a blind eye to pups eating other animals' poos.

You take your pup to preschool for six weeks, at the end of which you (both) graduate. At the ceremony you have to walk the pup up to where the vet is standing, command it to sit and stay, and then, and only then, will the vet hand you your graduation diploma. Needless to say your pup is the only one out of the twenty assorted mutts present who takes ten minutes to sit, and by then neither the vet nor the assembled owners are worried whether it stays or not. All they want is for you and your pup to leave. As soon as possible. Before the nineteen pups start eating each other's poo because they're so bored. So for God's sake give her the graduation diploma and let's get this show on the road.

Of course the pup has had such a good time at Puppy Preschool that, every time it comes within a kilometre of the vet's, it begins screeching and whining and pulling on the lead, heading for that place which is forever enshrined in its peabrain as a heaven on earth for pups. Forever, though, lasts only until the first time the pup has to go to the vet for some expensive nail-paring attention. The pup then realises it has made a terrible error of judgement, and from then on, whenever it comes within a kilometre of the vet's, it begins pulling the other way, making such a song and dance that people ring the SPCA and complain about cruelty to animals.

When you get a kitten it goes straight to the vet for an examination, injections, and (usually expensive) doses of vitamins. The mothers of the kittens you acquire are always short on these, it seems, and naturally have passed on this defect to their offspring. I think kittens should come with a tag saying Calcium Alert! or similar. You name it, they're always short of some crucial necessity. Thank God there's no such thing as Kitty Preschool. You see enough of the vet as it is. You've got to the stage where you're thinking seriously of filling in an automatic payment form at the bank and paying the vet a retainer.

The peculiar thing is that, if you haven't seen the vet for a week, you start getting withdrawal symptoms. The pets are perfectly okay — no fleas, no rashes, no worms, no vomiting, no eating problems, no cat bites, no dog bites, no psychological traumas (at least none you intend to do anything about). But still, you seem to end up at the vet's. It's become an addiction. But of course you don't call it that. You say, maybe the dog needs another piece of rawhide; or the cat needs a new bowl with the words Cat Dish emblazoned on the outside, and a picture of a cat on the inside — for stupid owners, or very intelligent cats, I presume. Or a new bag of multi-vitamin scientifically prepared all-purpose dietary top-notch ingredients guaranteed to put a shine on the coat and a smile on the face. Of the pet. The owner's face is rather glum as she wonders if she should ask the bank for an extension on her mortgage.

And then there are the accessories. Plastic feeding bowls, steel bowls, china bowls, and bowls with cartoons on them. Red leads, blue leads, green leads, as well as ordinary old black and brown; in leather, nylon, and string. Collars of all shapes and sizes. Toys for cats and toys for dogs. Tasty Training Treats which succeed only in training the dog to whine whenever it sees the packet. There are kennels, indoor and outdoor; flea powders, lotions, pills, herbal shampoos, deodorants, ointments for rashes and the ubiquitous evening primrose lotion. And there are the pet beds. Beds for every dog, from chihuahua to St Bernard. Because everyone knows dogs like to sleep up high. Like on the best couch. Although they'll make do with the newly planted-out bed of *Phlox drummondii,* at a pinch.

One day I saw this neat little bed, like a small bunk, with a tartan cover (Gay Gordon maybe?) and blue chrome legs. And it was Marked Down. Perfect: just the thing to stop the dog getting up on the couch. Most of the day the dog sleeps at my feet; but when my feet aren't available she persists in getting up on the couch. Which means I have to get very Spanish with a rolled-up newspaper. Which is a pain. Hence my interest in the bed.

Nights are no problem. At night she sleeps in a rather nice black wire indoor kennel — in fact, she puts herself to bed in it. But not during the day. During the day it's my feet or the couch.

I took the little bed home and put it in the middle of the sitting-room floor. We admired it. Very smart, very chic. Just the thing for the dog who likes a bit of style. I lift her up and put her on it. 'Nice bed,' I say. She gets straight down. I put her on the bed. 'Sit,' I say. She sits briefly, two seconds perhaps, then gets down. 'Good dog,' I say, wilfully overlooking the fact that this expression is probably the best oxymoron of all time; but hey, needs must. She wags her tail. 'Up, up,' I say. She looks at me. Looks at the dear little tartan-covered, blue-chrome comfortable modern dog chaise longue, gives it the doggy equivalent of 'bugger that', and trots outside.

During the next week I place the dog bed by the ranchslider, by the couch, in front of the television, under the table, in my office, in the garden. The dog pretends not to see it. I am consumed with remorse over spending good money on this latest accessory — the last in a long line of such purchases. I do not, it seems, want to learn that such items are made to attract owners, not pets.

I give up on the dog and try to persuade the cat that it would like this dear little bed better than the decrepit scratched old cane stool it sleeps on. It refuses to listen. In the end I admit defeat. The trouble with our pets is that they're too well treated. Dogs in the Third World would be ecstatic if offered such a wonderful little bed to sleep on. As for cats, they'd gladly forsake their piece of dry old earth to snuggle up on this magnificent piece of pet furniture.

I store the dear little tartan-covered blue-chrome-legged bed under my desk.

Along with:

- the red knitted Arran Doggie-Design Waistcoat, the collars with silver chiming bells on it so you'll always know where your pet is (which sends the pet into hysterics every time it comes within a few feet of it),
- the rare South American striped flea collar and lead,
- the yellow plastic raincoat,
- the superduper artificial bone guaranteed to strengthen jaw muscles and encourage proper chewing,
- the grey fur mouse stuffed with catnip,
- the Cosy Clean and Comfie Cat Hidey-Hole lined with lambswool and with its own built-in purr encourager . . .

'Just face it,' says my Significant Other rather tersely, 'you are the only pet accessory they need or want.' Gee thanks.

NEW YEAR'S REVOLUTIONS III

Dogs whose owners allow them to poo on beaches will be trained to bite the hand that feeds them.

Cat-owners who don't spay their female cats will be forced to work at the SPCA every Saturday for a year.

Someone will invent a toaster that toasts *every corner* of a slice of bread, I mean *each side at once, Buster.* In thirty seconds.

All women with wrinkles and a few rolls around their middle will be seen as desirable, intelligent, witty — and not just by cats.

Grey Power will change its name to Super Seniors and will be composed of people who welcome other people over sixty even if they are queer.

The night Mrs Ernie went 10 no trumps

I've always gone along with being partners with Mrs Ernie when Reet and Ernie and me have a game of 500. I mean, what can a man do? It's sort of expected, you know, when you're neighbours and you get together on the odd Saturday night for a game. And she's not exactly a bad player. In fact when she's got four aces, the joker, and a run of something she does pretty well.

Mrs Ernie's never quite grasped that there's more to playing cards than just putting down the joker, four aces, and a good run. Any fool can win a hand that way. It's the one who goes 7 diamonds and gets them, when all they started with was the joker, the ace and a couple of rags. It's all in the way you play.

You know when you bid 6 no trumps to let your partner know you've got the joker? And then they bid back 7 hearts to let you know they've got the ace of hearts? Mrs Ernie says that's cheating. That's not cheating. It's a well established system of playing. But she won't be convinced. And she's a neighbour and not a bad sort of woman, so what can you do?

Last Saturday night we all got settled, a dish of Reet's salted peanuts to hand, a glass of Tui for Ernie and me and a glass of medium golden sherry for Reet and Mrs Ernie. We cut for deal and Ernie won. He dealt the cards, and hardly had he slapped down the last card on the kitty when Mrs Ernie says, quite loudly, 10 no trumps. Ernie and Reet stared at her but I nearly fell off my chair. You see I'd had a quick shufti at my hand and I had the joker.

I didn't quite know what to do. Or say. How does anyone bid 10 no trumps without the joker? And Mrs Ernie of all people? Sure, I was her partner, but she didn't know I had the joker when she bid, did she? It could just as easily have been Reet or Ernie. Something wrong here, Tom, I thought. I glanced over at Reet. She rolled her eyes. Something was definitely up. Loud and clear. I have a long experience of Reet's eye-rolling and that was the message from this one, no doubt about it.

Ernie cleared his throat. 'Ten no trumps eh,' he said.

'Something wrong with that?' Mrs Ernie sounded quite put out.

Ernie shook his head. 'No,' he says, 'course not.'

'I might not be as "adventurous" as Maeve Fritter,' she said, 'but if I want to go 10 no trumps there's no law against it, is there?'

'I told you,' Ernie mumbled. 'I didn't mean anything.'

Mrs Ernie threw her cards down and they splayed all over the table and a couple slid over the edge and onto the floor. 'That's what you say now,' she said. She stood up, picked up the sherry, drained it and threw the glass over her shoulder. Fortunately it landed on the carpet. 'There,' said Mrs Ernie. 'Is that dramatic enough for you?' She leaned over, picked up Ernie's beer and tipped it over his head. Then she looked at Reet and me. 'Sorry Reet, sorry Tom,' she said. 'I'm a bit upset. I'd better go.'

'Now hang on,' said Reet. She gestured at me and I went and got a flannel and a towel from the bathroom and handed them to Ernie. I must admit he looked a bit of a ningnong sitting there with beer dripping down his face.

'What say I make a cup of tea,' Reet says to Mrs Ernie. 'Nice and strong. And you and Ernie sit down and have a talk. Things can often be sorted out with a talk.'

'Some things can't be sorted that easily,' Mrs Ernie said, but she stayed. I think she felt a bit better. You know how you do when you let it go a bit? I know some people think you should keep things bottled up, but Reet always reckons there's a time and a place. She says we're all time bombs really, and sometimes you get rid of a lot of steam and avoid a really big explosion if you just let it rip occasionally. It's like everything else though, Reet says, okay if you don't overdo it.

I took the towel and flannel from Ernie and showed him through to the bathroom. While he was cleaning himself up I put some cold water in the washhouse tub and dropped the dirty towel and flannel in it. Obviously Ernie and Mrs Ernie had some things to sort out, but at our place? Over a game of 500? And what about that mention of Maeve Fritter? What'd she have to do with anything?

Maeve Fritter was the new schoolteacher. A nice enough girl as far as I knew. Good with the kids. Doesn't put up with any nonsense, expects homework on time, but they seem to like her. The wagging had gone right down. But what has Maeve Fritter got to do with Ernie? Shit, I thought, Deep Waters, Tom.

When I got back to the sitting room, Reet was pouring water into the teapot and Mrs Ernie was blowing her nose. Ernie looked at me. I looked at Ernie. Then we looked away.

I started picking up the cards. I had a quick look as I set them together. Looked to me as though Mrs Ernie might have been stretching it to get even 6 no trumps, because when I picked up Reet's hand I saw she had two aces, and when I looked at Ernie's, he had one. And I'd had the other one. But I didn't say anything. I quickly shuffled the cards and put them back in their packet.

'I hear you're going to act in a play Ernie,' said Reet.

Ernie looked as though he could have sunk through the floor. 'Thinking about it,' he said, 'just thinking about it.'

You could've knocked me down with a feather. Ernie in a play? I mean I like Ernie, and I'd be the first one to admit that you'd have to go far to find a better neighbour but even with the best will in the world, I'd have to say he's no oil painting.

I saw it all now. Maeve Fritter must be wanting to put on a play with adults in it for a change. And she must've asked Ernie to go in it. And Mrs Ernie didn't like it. To put it mildly.

'Have you ever acted in a play?' Reet asked Mrs Ernie.

Mrs Ernie's lips curled. She shook her head. 'I don't suppose I'm "adventurous" enough,' she said.

Ernie sighed. 'All I meant was, it's the first time someone's put on a play here. Apart from CWI of course. But they're all women. And this is going to have some men in it.'

'I bet,' said Mrs Ernie.

Reet turned her head and rolled her eyes at me. Okay, I thought, hope she knows what she's doing.

'If anyone asked me,' I said, 'I'd have to say that I think you're very adventurous, Mrs Ernie.'

Reet nodded. Mrs Ernie's mouth dropped. Just like they say mouths do in books. I'd never seen anyone actually do it in cold blood before.

'Well,' I said, 'Ernie nearly lost you when he set fire to the back of the house, and then you nearly sent yourself blind by splashing marigold juice on your eyes. Don't know about you, but that's what I call adventurous.'

'Me too,' says Ernie, quickly.

Take it easy Ernie, I thought, no need to overdo it.

Mrs Ernie let out a big breath. 'Well,' she says, 'well.' But she was pleased, I could tell.

Reet said, 'I did hear Maeve Fritter was looking for someone to be Prompt. She said it's got to be someone who knows what they're doing and won't take any nonsense. Because the whole play depends on them. Don't suppose you'd be interested?'

Mrs Ernie pursed her lips and didn't speak.

Reet said, 'It might suit you because you'll be hearing Ernie's lines anyway, won't you, so you'll have a fair idea of who says what, where.'

'I could think about it I suppose,' says Mrs Ernie, finally.

Home and hosed, I thought. Good old Reet. I stirred my tea. 'Okay Tom,' said Reet, 'you'll have the spoon through the bottom if you're not careful.'

Later, after the dishes were done and we were sitting in the sitting room, Reet says, 'How about getting us a sherry, Tom?'

'Bit late isn't it?'

Reet looked at me.

I looked back at her.

'I'm in the mood to be "adventurous",' she said. And she grins.

I could feel a big stupid grin taking over my face. 'You're on,' I said.

Travelling with Renée

All roads lead to Woodville, but some of them take a bloody long time to get there.

Is there a good reason for the lack of signs indicating how you get to the Manawatu Gorge? Or is it just being an OAP *and* a woman that makes it difficult?

When we finally found the Manawatu Gorge we were one of three lucky vehicles behind a three-tier sheep truck. Almost immediately, like in a flash, we noticed that the top tier gate had slid open about a third and a sheep was poking its head out, threatening to jump. The driver of the van behind the truck, which had DOG KENNELS printed on it, beeped at the truck driver and made signs. Obviously the driver of the Dog Kennels van knew what the signs meant, but alas, the driver of the sheep truck didn't. As the signs got more frantic the truck driver put his foot down in an attempt to get away from this menace at the back of him. Someone who'd forgotten to take their medication. Shouldn't be allowed to hold a driver's licence.

The driver of the stationwagon behind the Dog Kennels van, which had EVENING STANDARD on it, was, like us no doubt, trying to keep from driving over the edge of the winding gorge and at the same time keep a watch on the sheep who might miss the Dog Kennels van and land, kerplunk splat, on the *Evening Standard* stationwagon. Or, even more horrifying from my point of view — and in these situations it's all me me me, isn't it? — it might miss the Dog Kennel van *and* the *Evening Standard* stationwagon and land, kerplunk splat, on our blank Honda Accord. An older model, perhaps, but we love it because it keeps going.

The Manawatu Gorge takes about seven minutes at the most to drive through these days. The sheep, I presume the same one, kept advancing to the hole, taking a quick shufti at us, then backing off. I don't know why. In fact I don't know anything about sheep. This is probably a fault in a country like New Zealand, but hey, you can't know everything.

The Dog Kennels van driver kept up his signalling and the truck driver kept driving. I kept up a steady stream of Oh God, Oh no, Don't do it Julie, Holy shit, things like that, while my Significant Other drove, muttering to herself about bloody male drivers who wouldn't understand bloody signals if they got up and bloody bit them. What the woman driving the *Evening Standard* stationwagon was doing is anyone's guess. Praying? Or ringing through to the newsroom to give in her notice, perhaps.

Seven years passed, and with hysteria levels (I'm serious — I couldn't stop laughing), at least in the Honda, at an all-time high, we drove out of the gorge. The Dog Kennels van driver leaned on his accelerator and passed the sheep truck. His horn blared and he and his passenger gesticulated wildly at the truck driver. The Dog Kennels van cut in front of the sheep truck and parked on the side of the road. The sheep truck passed it and continued driving. Congratulating himself. Thank God I've got rid of that idiot.

They're everywhere these days.

The sheep's head and shoulders leaned out. Shit, I gibbered, it's not choosing to jump, it's being pushed! Maybe the others are sick of its company. Maybe it wouldn't stop baaing, maybe that could get boring on a long trip. Well I don't know, do I?

The *Evening Standard* stationwagon driver slowed. Poor thing, how was she coping on her own, with no support? No one to gibber to.

We slowed.

And finally, the sheep truck driver decided, Oh well, better humour these ningnongs. He curved over to the side of the road. Better find out what all the fuss was about. I mean, one crazy driver behind him is believable, but three?

The Dog Kennels van driver, a broken man, just stayed where he was wiping his face. Let the whole bloody lot jump, he was possibly saying, see if I care. The Dog Kennels van passenger, though, was made of sterner stuff. He leaped out and ran towards the truck driver, who backed away and began some rather erratic signalling of his own.

The woman driving the *Evening Standard* stationwagon had the right idea. She picked up speed and drove like hell. At the first garage she whipped in, screeched to a halt and sprinted for the toilets. Women's or men's, who cares? Let's liberate the men's. I'm just in the mood for a confrontation.

We tooted to show solidarity, and kept driving. I started thinking: I mean, at times like this you have to ask yourself, is it me? But after about 100 kilometres, into the heavy silence, I got it. Jeez, I said, maybe that's why they don't have any signs telling you where the Manawatu Gorge is.

Is it Me?

I think there should be a time limit on cash machines. Anyone who takes longer than a minute should be stripped of all their medals. Or put in the stocks for a week. Or shot. Travellers always need cash. And when travellers line up at the cash machine the person in front is always playing Beethoven's Fifth and he just can't get that quaver right so he has to stop and start all over again. Sorry, he calls, with a wide smile. But I don't smile back. My smiles don't come cheap.

In the motel a woman is screaming. It is late at night. I ring 111. Ring Noise Control, I am told. I mean, really, it *is* me, isn't it.

What kind of person steals jamjars off graves? I'll tell you. Someone who has bought three bunches of flowers to share out between Rose and Gertrude — God knows there'll be trouble if one gets one more rosebud than the other — gets to their graves and finds some bugger has stolen the jamjars which they left there last time they visited.

Why is it that, whenever we travel on the ferry between the North and South Islands on a day when the sea is not like a millpond, we always strike someone who sits down beside us and wants to tell us in full Technicolor detail about the day his grandfather travelled on the *Wahine*? He tells us how the waves were so high, the winds were gale force; how the ferry struck the rocks just in sight of home, capsized and lots of people drowned, amongst whom was the aforementioned grandfather. Look, it's not that I'm devoid of compassion. I empathise, I do, with his distress at the memories that being on the ferry evokes. But why the hell does he have to pick me? As well as not being devoid of compassion, I also am not devoid of imagination. Even when the sea is like a millpond, I see us crashing into the rocks, being dashed into the boiling sea, hundreds of heads floating in the water fighting over pieces of wood, hands upstretched, Hey over *here*! I'm not waving, I'm *drowning*, you fool! I mean, it *is* me, isn't it?

Overheard in a café: *Yeah, we like travelling, but we went to South Africa and there was nothing there.* See? It's not me. Or if it is, I'm not the only one.

HOUSEWORK WITH RENÉE II

A job I hate hate HATE is 'doing the bookshelves'. For some inscrutable reason, between the last time I 'did the bookshelves' and this time, the books have rearranged themselves into unalphabetical order. Which means they have to be rearranged in alphabetical order. Well, otherwise I'd never find the one I want when I want it, would I?

The moment I've got the books from every bookshelf lying in rows on couches, tables, floors, stairs, chairs, the doorbell rings. *Hello! Thought we'd surprise you!* Well you did that all right.

Where does all the gunk that adheres to the oven sides, bottom and top, come from?

I think I'll shift.

When I tell you I've got breast cancer . . .

Do not scream and back away saying, *No no no.* I know it presents you with intimations of your own mortality, but so does walking across a pedestrian crossing.

Do not immediately lower your voice and speak to me as though I'm going to cark it at any moment. Perhaps it makes you feel healthier and stronger to see me as weaker and more fragile, but do not be surprised if I tell you to piss off.

Do not tell me about your auntie who died recently of breast cancer. Or I might tell you of the sudden death by strangulation of someone who told someone who had a breast cancer that their auntie had recently died of a breast cancer.

Remember a lump is a lump is a lump, so do not ask me how big the lump is.

Do not tell me you think it's awful that the government has not followed through with the breast cancer screening programme they promised. The government has not followed through on lots of promises. That's what governments do.

Do not tell me about this book you read where it was proved that cancer is caused by stress. Because murder is also often caused by stress.

When you ask me how we are, and I say, 'She's got laryngitis and I've got a breast cancer but apart from that we're okay, thank you for asking,' I expect you to laugh.

Do not mention nature cures where the main emphasis seems to be on the patient's ability to heal themselves. So that if I don't get cured, it's all my fault: I didn't try hard enough.

Instead . . .

How about popping round with a bottle of a nice Gewürztraminer, which is my fav at the moment, and telling me some juicy gossip about a Member of Parliament and a journalist? You don't know any? Look, ask around, there's always gossip about a Member of Parliament and a journalist. Believe me.

Say, how about a picnic at Butterfly Creek on Sunday afternoon? It's a pretty steep climb but I know you won't offer to carry my backpack.

Ring me up and tell me about the sixtieth birthday party where the ninety-year-old mother got up and did a fantastic tango with her daughter.

Send me a beautiful red lily you saw that reminded you of me.

Write to me and say you're sorry to hear the news, you know I'll be okay, and would I like to think about doing a walking tour of England in July?

Send me a card and and give me the number of two friends of yours who have both had breast cancer and are now (a) climbing mountains, and (b) power walking.

Tell me all you know about the surgeon and his amazing skill.

Make me laugh by telling me about the latest lesbian craze.

Send me an invitation to a celebration of Paul Robeson's life.

Ask me how my work's going.

And when I cry, cry with me.

Bibliography

The Bible (Modern, Revised, Unplugged) by Peter, Paul and Mary.

The Community Unconscious by Siggie Jung.

How to Have Constructive Arguments When One of You is a Writer by Ernest H. Way.

The Woman's Dictionary of Handy Myths, Secrets & Lies by Germaine Gloria Smith.

Every Man's Collection of Handy Myths, Secrets & Lies by the Matthew, Mark, Luke and John Fishing Corporation, Inc.

Organics, Organisms, Orgasms: On the Road to Bluff, with Bill Throw.